LEAD THE FUTURE

THE 12 SKILLS TO LEAD IN A FAST CHANGING & AMBIGUOUS WORLD

JESSICA SCHUBERT

"Beyond insightful and incredibly timely! As the world starts to look forward, and we as leaders begin the arduous task of leading our teams post-pandemic, only one thing is guaranteed – change and uncertainty will be constants.

Coming from the aviation sector that has been heavily impacted by the Covid crisis, I have applied the '12 Skills' in this book into my own leadership approach, particularly over the last 18 months. These skills have become my cornerstones in leading people thoughtfully and delivering strategies for the business that create agility, drive change and embrace innovation – all ultimately moving our business forward, beyond the crisis and into the future.

Jess's book is a "must read" for any leader!"

—NOELLA FERNS: HEAD OF SALES ASIA PACIFIC, BRITISH AIRWAYS & IBERIA AIRLINES

"...a fascinating and practical read. Jessica's key message on 'Leadership and Self' is spot-on. In times of uncertainty and accelerating technological change, a focus on 'Strength-based Leadership', 'Courage & Resilience' and 'Emotional Intelligence' are critical guiding principles in one's career journey."

—LI LOW: DIRECTOR, EY WAVESPACE™

"A timely, valuable combination of deep insight and research, with practical advice for leaders. This book is relevant, smart and helpful for immediate challenges, but also to strengthen the foundations to succeed in the future."

—LYN HAWKINS: NATIONAL DIRECTOR, BUSINESS WOMEN AUSTRALIA.

"Jessica Schubert has written a must-read leadership guide for the 21st century. If you are looking for an edge with your leadership team then this is a must-read book. Jessica highlights how the speed of change puts a focus on the skills that matter so that leaders are empowered and capable of leading now rather than catching up with the future. Learn from one of the best up-and-coming leadership coaches in Australasia."

—LACHLAN SLOAN: COFOUNDER, 505 LABS

"The global pandemic has accelerated the need for leaders who are more responsive to the needs of others, evolving technology and customer behaviour. Jessica's '12 leadership skills' provide tangible reference points developed from experience working with leadership teams globally, and they work!"

—ROZANNE KIDD: DIRECTOR, RURAL PAYMENTS AGENCY, DEFRA UK

"*Lead the Future* gives you an excellent overview of what is important right now and what will be important in the future to be a successful leader. The Covid-19 crisis has accelerated the need to master the 'new way of working', and this book is full of relevant case studies and best practice. *Lead the Future* helped me personally to develop the skills I need to thrive in a fast-changing and challenging business world."

—MICHAEL DROTLEFF: CHIEF COMMERCIAL OFFICER, SPONSOO, GERMANY

"I had the pleasure and honour of working with Jessica in the past and I'm beyond thrilled about this book!! Jessica has always shown such exceptional leadership and coaching skills, working alongside leaders from all across the world for 20+ years and she's FINALLY sharing all her wise knowledge in this must-read "bible" about the future of leadership in this ever-changing world. All I can say is read this book to learn from one of the best!"

—LINDA FELGENTREFF: GLOBAL SALES MANAGER KEY ACCOUNTS, ADP FRANCE

'THE ILLITERATE OF THE 21ST CENTURY WILL NOT BE THOSE WHO CANNOT READ AND WRITE, BUT THOSE WHO CANNOT LEARN, UNLEARN, AND RELEARN.'

—ALVIN TOFFLER

Published by Jessica Schubert
Melbourne, Australia
Contact www.intactteams.com

© 2021 Jessica Schubert

Author: Jessica Schubert
Title: Lead The Future: The 12 Skills to Lead in a Fast Changing & Ambiguous World
ISBN: 9780645265903
Subjects: Leadership | Management | Business
Book production services: www.smartwomenpublish.com
Book cover design: Celine David

NATIONAL LIBRARY OF AUSTRALIA

A catalogue record for this book is available from the National Library of Australia

Disclaimer:

CONTENTS

Introduction   The World Has Changed 3

Chapter 1   Why Leading the Future Matters Now 9

        VUCA is Our Reality. 10

        The 5 Megatrends. 13

        Impact on Workplaces and Leadership 38

        Megatrends: Complexity, Pace, Connectivity 39

Chapter 2   Where Are You on the Journey

        to Lead the Future? 47

        From Following to Leading the Future. 50

        Team-Member Engagement Model 51

Chapter 3   The Four Stages of Leading the Future. 77

        The 4 Pillars of Leadership. 79

Chapter 4   The 12 Skills Needed to Lead the Future 87

        Skill 1: Strength-based Leadership 89

        Skill 2: Courage and Resilience 94

        Skill 3: Emotional Intelligence 105

        Skill 4: Communicating and Influencing 110

        Skill 5: Feedback and Productive Conflict 120

        Skill 6: Leading in a Hybrid World. 133

        Skill 7: Agility and Change Management 146

        Skill 8: Complex Problem-solving 151

        Skill 9: Adaptability 156

        Skill 10: Embrace Technology 160

        Skill 11: Vision and Foresight. 164

        Skill 12: Mobilise 165

Conclusion   171

Work with Jessica 173

Endnotes   175

INTRODUCTION

THE WORLD HAS CHANGED

On the morning of Friday, 13 March 2020, I had a call with the CEO of Business Women Australia (BWA), Lyn Hawkins. 'What are we going to do with the workshop I'm facilitating next week for forty people?' I asked her.

The World Health Organisation had officially characterised Covid-19 as a pandemic only two days prior to this, and while the Australian Federal Government had yet to release official social restrictions, it didn't feel right to be hosting a large gathering amid this pandemic.

It had already been a strange couple of weeks. I was still working part time for an organisation based in Europe, taking post-graduate students on experiential international study programs. At the time I was hosting a group of students and professors from Alabama in my home city of Melbourne, but just two days into the study tour the university decided to bring all students and staff who were on trips or study abroad back home due to fear the United States might soon close its borders.

I remember feeling a real shift in energy when saying goodbye to the group. Afterwards I dropped off gifts to the cancelled speakers, with my apologies. Everyone seemed on edge, people were keeping their distance, and organisations started hastily preparing for social-distancing regulations and check-ins at reception.

On Sunday, 15 March we decided we had to cancel the BWA in-house event and instead facilitate it on Zoom. When I ended my call with Lyn, I stared at my computer. I knew this was a pivotal moment; it was clear the world would never be the same.

The following days felt like a bit of a blur. I remember talking to friends and family members more frequently than usual, discussing what was happening and analysing the information we had access to. I was listening to the news 24/7, yearning for clarity, explanations, a plan. Then clients started to cancel or postpone workshops and coaching sessions, and within a matter of days I was faced with the prospect of having very little paid work. Sunday, 15 March 2020 goes down for me as one of the most significant and terrifying days of my life. It was obvious: the pandemic did not discriminate, it was here to stay for a while, and it would impact each and every one of us.

It took me a few days of little sleep and growing anxiety, but at the end of March I got up one morning, grabbed my notebook and made a plan for navigating the next few months. After looking at my financials I realised that even the worst-case scenario would actually see me through a number of months, which immediately put me at ease. Plus, I knew I could keep working with my clients using online platforms. After all, we had just facilitated the BWA event on Zoom and it had worked well.

I also thought about what my clients and other leaders would need from me, and the first thing I did was reach out to them. I picked up the phone and had conversations with leaders all over the world to find out how the pandemic was impacting them and their teams, what they were struggling with personally, and how I could help. These weren't sales calls, just reach-out calls, because I knew that if I were struggling with this lingering uncertainty and ambiguity my clients would be, too.

Over the next few weeks every country in which I have clients went into some form of lockdown. Some organisations, especially in the tourism, aviation and education industries, scaled back operations significantly. Other industries like hospitality and retail quickly shifted their business models to online purchasing, and most companies moved whole workforces out of their offices and into their homes.

The world as we know it changed in early 2020. Every country, and in fact every individual, has experienced the pandemic differently. The rules around lockdowns and social restrictions, and health advice and decisions from each government around the world have all varied greatly, and still do differ. At the time of writing, vaccines are being rolled out in many countries, but there's still a long way to go for the world collectively before there is some form of normality again.

Australia's strategy has been to suppress the virus. I live in Melbourne, which, after infection rates skyrocketed in July 2020, imposed one of the longest and strictest second lockdowns; we were effectively put into a type of protective custody. We were in lockdown for one hundred and ten days, and were allowed out only one hour per day for exercise, food shopping or medical care. We could travel within a 5-kilometre radius of home only, and a curfew was imposed from eight pm to five am.

We had to get used to working from home and home-schooling children. We couldn't visit our loved ones, and many people worried about their elderly parents or grandparents. We had no timeline for when the restrictions would be lifted, and this uncertainty was tough on most people's mental health.

After going through this tough lockdown, I have real empathy for every country and individual who has had a similar experience, with its associated social disconnect, fear of the unknown, and the lack of control that comes with being dependent on what the government will decide in the near future.

What the last eighteen months have taught me is that human beings are extremely adaptable and resilient. I learned new ways of connecting with my clients and facilitating conversations. I realised how important my deep friendships are, and how quickly people will rally in support of those in need.

Through hundreds of conversations with my clients and my wider network of associates I realised that change had been on the way for some time. The pandemic had simply accelerated the need to rethink how we organise our work and lead our people.

I had been leading cross-cultural teams in the corporate sector all across the Asia–Pacific region since the turn of the century, before I decided to launch my own coaching and leadership practice in 2013. I have worked with leaders from every walk of life, from different continents and industries, with different backgrounds and levels of experience. I have helped hundreds of people become better leaders, realise their potential, and head up their own teams and organisations.

The fundamentals of leadership haven't changed. A leader's job is to guide their people, communicate and coach, encourage teamwork and collaboration, give feedback and offer solutions, delegate and set expectations, and manage risk responsibly. What *has* changed is the landscape: specifically, the mode of working and the pace at which the world works.

In 2020, I realised that in a matter of weeks the world had not only changed, but it had changed for good. Life will not return to the way it was. Instead, our mission as leaders is to guide our people through this pandemic to whatever lies beyond, from an organisational point of view as well as from the perspective of giving personal support.

Change is happening and it's happening fast. Automation, disruption and our new reality of a VUCA (Volatility, Uncertainty, Complexity and Ambiguity) world have put a huge amount of pressure on leaders, but on the positive side we now have opportunities to create more flexibility in the workplace and renew purpose in organisations.

Technological disruption is shaping the future of work and it's clear that while many people think machines will take our jobs, it is human skills that count. The 2016 World Economic Forum's 'The Future of Jobs' report states: 'The current technological revolution need not become a race between humans and machines, but rather an opportunity for work to truly become a channel through which people recognise their full potential.' This statement has become even truer now in 2021 as I write this. We need a focus on leadership skills that matter *now* so leaders are empowered and capable of leading rather than simply catching up with the future of work. The future of work is forming now.

I believe that we have lost our focus on people through our obsession with technological advancement and digitalisation. We need to look at how we organise our work and structure our workplaces in this new, hybrid world, but we also need to go back to human skills. We are currently working through a transition phase, which has been termed 'the new normal' or 'the next normal'.

In this phase, I see a real opportunity for leaders and organisations to reconnect to a new purpose by creating workplace cultures that are fit for this purpose, and equipping workforces with the skills that matter to navigate this fast-changing and ambiguous world. Being successful in the future is not just about leadership anymore; it's about leading the future.

This book is not just about the Covid-19 pandemic, and nor is it focused solely on the future of work, although we can't ignore outside factors, social markers and global developments as they impact the way we work, lead and make decisions. *Lead the Future* is a book for people who lead teams, departments or organisations, and who want to learn how to navigate ongoing uncertainty, make good decisions in a rapidly changing environment, and be the best leaders they can be.

I wrote this book because I want to share the stories I hear in my coaching sessions and in my conversations with leaders. These conversations, and the stories my clients tell of their great successes and epic fails, provide context for what the world looks like right now and for what the future holds.

Lead the Future will give you insights into 5 Megatrends that will help you understand what is happening in the world right now. I have collected data, research, stories and wisdom. I have designed training sessions, online webinars and keynote presentations to help leaders become better leaders. I have taken all this information and learning, and developed the framework for the 12 Skills that will help you lead in a dynamic and uncertain environment.

It's time to *lead the future*.

CHAPTER 1

WHY LEADING THE FUTURE MATTERS NOW

I want to give you some background to the reality we live in. You might have heard the expression, 'We live in a VUCA world'. These words don't just ring true because of the Covid-19 pandemic; the VUCA (Volatility, Uncertainty, Complexity, Ambiguity) world has existed for much longer. I first heard the term when I moved to Hong Kong in 2010, but it was originally coined by Warren Bennis and Burt Nanus in 1987 and is based on their leadership theories.

> 'THE WORLD IS CHANGING VERY FAST. BIG WILL NOT BEAT SMALL ANYMORE. IT WILL BE THE FAST BEATING THE SLOW.'
>
> —RUPERT MURDOCH

VUCA IS OUR REALITY

Living in a VUCA world means being exposed to fast, unprecedented changes in markets or industries through disruption, industry dynamism, and fluctuation in demand. Just look at the rise of Netflix, Uber and Airbnb, and the way the world consumes entertainment, transportation and accommodation. The more volatile the world, the faster will be the change. Uncertainty comes from not being able to predict the future, either because we're unaware of what's happening around us or because the future is not actually predictable.

When changes and circumstances are complex, it's challenging to analyse and predict the future, especially when it comes to technological advances. There are so many factors to consider that organisations lose themselves in the complexity. Interpreting situations so we can make sense of them and relate them to our challenges and plans is important for future-proofing our businesses, but information can be incomplete, vague or hypothetical. Instead of clarity we're often faced with ambiguity, which can lead to a lack of confidence in making good decisions.[1]

One of the most poignant VUCA events has been the Covid-19 pandemic, which has impacted every human in every corner of the world. The way that many of us live and work changed within weeks, countless people lost their freedom, and far too many people lost their lives. The frightening part was, and remains so as I write, that the future is still hard to predict, and new information about virus mutations and vaccines keeps governments and businesses in uncertainty. Working with professionals all over the world, I have noticed that decision-making has become a lot more challenging for leaders.

The 21st century had already had its fair share of VUCA incidents. I remember the dot-com crash at the beginning of the century, when I had just moved from Germany to Australia, and the global financial crisis in 2008, which left many citizens on the brink of their financial existence.

Environmental disasters have also had a huge impact. I moved to Japan in 2011, after the earthquake and Fukushima incident, and I witnessed how devastated the whole country was; indeed, Japan is still recovering today. Living in Australia, I am exposed to devastating bushfires every year. I remember the Black Saturday bushfires in February 2007, feeling the ash on my skin and taste on my tongue, when we lost one hundred and seventy-three citizens.

Environmental disasters, health crises, wars, and technological advancements continue to impact the world. The pace of incidents has seemed to accelerate, giving us a feeling of being in an almost constant VUCA state.

The question for leaders is: how do we navigate the challenges to ensure our employees continue to be safe, optimistic and productive? Also, how can we ensure that we don't get left behind? For many businesses, technological advancement—especially automation and artificial intelligence—is the greatest threat to their structure or existence. The digital revolution is in full swing, and people are afraid that machines will take their jobs. And although we have been operating in a VUCA world for a while, the pace of change keeps accelerating.

In his book, *Impact*, Paul Gibbons paints a clear picture: 'Moore's Law doubles computations power every two years, but few people have put serious thought into how humans stay competitive as machines get smarter.'

Global incidents are drivers of change, and they are not all devastating. Technological advancement has opened up live-changing opportunities for individuals and businesses. Just look at the rise of FANGA (Facebook, Amazon, Netflix, Google and Apple) and the pace at which these organisations have grown and changed the world.

So the pace of change is accelerating and that is going to continue. What has also changed is connectivity. Globalisation and digitalisation have enabled us to live and work in an ultra-connected world. Imagine if Covid-19 had happened in the 1980s.

Businesses are being impacted by change that's out of their control. The way we live, consume and work has changed, and as leaders we are a crucial part of that. As leaders, we need to be able to identify the challenges and opportunities that a globalised, fast-changing world presents.

I have identified 5 main drivers of change, which I call megatrends. These 5 Megatrends are important for everyone, and crucial in shaping leaders' realities.

THE 5 MEGATRENDS

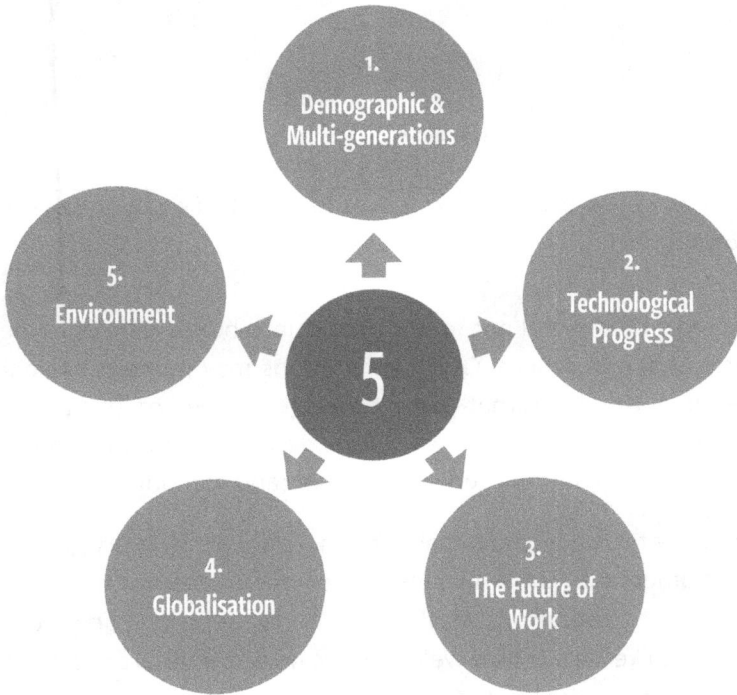

The 5 Megatrends affecting organisations and leaders in the 21st century

Megatrend 1: Demographics and Multi-generations

Millennials are so entitled. They don't have the same work ethic as us.
Do those words sound familiar? I hear these comments over and over
again from the older generation of leaders. And the problem is clear: new
generations have entered the workforce; they work differently and have
different priorities.

In many organisations these days, up to five generations work under
one roof. If we want to work together, we need to first understand any
fundamental differences and then find ways of working together towards
common goals.

Builders	Baby Boomers	Generation X	Gen Y Millennials	Generation Z	Generation Alpha
Born <1946	Born 1946-64	Born 1965-79	Born 1980-94	Born 1995-09	Born 2010-24

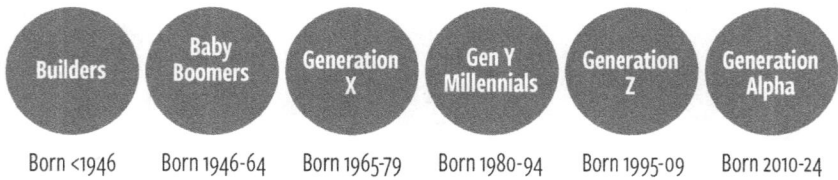

Generations by year of birth. Now the Greek alphabet is being used to avoid stereotypes.

We have to be mindful not to put people into boxes when it comes to generational differences. Older generations may perceive millennials as feeling entitled, but that doesn't mean every person born between 1980 and 1994 *is* actually that way. Some differences are easily observed and can give insight into general priorities and working styles.

It's important to understand that differences are felt by every generation. Baby boomers may think millennials are entitled and not hardworking, and younger generations may think older generations are too rigid. Comments like *This is how we've always done things around here* can make those who identify as Generation Z cringe; these younger people may have little tolerance for wasting resources like paper when it's possible to digitalise all processes.

I work with a private consulting firm in Australia. The senior executives are baby boomers, but the majority of their workforce, such as analysts and graduates, is made up of Generation Z. The leaders in the middle, mostly millennials, are trying to close the gap as the vision of the executive team—*Let's do things how we've always done them*—is vastly different to the way younger employees see the world, which could be summarised as: *Let's adapt to what our clients need and give us the freedom to do our jobs in the best way we can.*

One of the biggest misconceptions leaders have is that the behaviour of a younger generation is 'a fad'. The notion of *We'll recruit them, show them how to do things around here and then they'll grow out of it* won't work. It's not a pendulum. Behaviour in general is driven by our priorities and what we believe to be true, and is very closely connected to our values. Beliefs and values are shaped by the way we grow up. They help us decide what our priorities are and what we consider is the right thing to do. And we bring those values into the workplace.

I recall being in a room full of businesswomen in the finance industry who were talking about multi-generational leadership. This is what I said to the many baby boomers present: 'You complain about the typical traits of millennials, but remember that you brought them up; that generation is your children.'

Each generation is a product of events and leaders during their lives, their own development, their upbringing, their parents, their culture, the country they live in, and the trends of their time.

Historical events and trends of our time create something called social markers. Consider some of the social markers of baby boomers. They grew up in the time of the first TV, rock and roll, and the Cold War. Generation X grew up with the first personal computers in house-holds and was the first generation to have been widely brought up in single-parent families. Generation Y, aka millenials, grew up with the internet, cable TV, and opportunities for global internships. They have been born into a world of natural disasters and feel strongly about environmentalism. Generations Z and Alpha, who have been born into the digital world, are known as 'digital natives'.

It's important to understand the fundamental differences at play when people bring their values and priorities into a workplace. What comes next is to simply have conversations about those differences and any commonalities, and decide how to meet in the middle.

The graphic below gives an overview of generations in the workforce.[2]

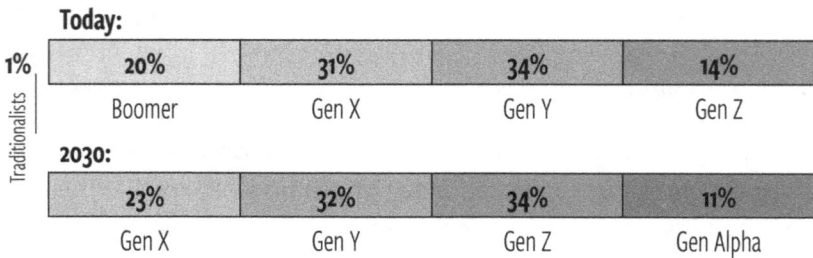

Today:

1%	20%	31%	34%	14%
	Boomer	Gen X	Gen Y	Gen Z

2030:

23%	32%	34%	11%
Gen X	Gen Y	Gen Z	Gen Alpha

Traditionalists

A comparison of the generational make-up of our workforce. By 2030, over 70% of workers will be Gen Y and younger.

Source: McCrindle 2019

In 2030, Generations Y and Z will make up seventy percent of the workforce, and it's our job right now to prepare them to be the best leaders they can be. We need to set up younger generations for success and together co-create the future of work. It's not about answering to a younger generation's every whim, but reaching organisational goals and delivering our work. Successful collaboration between generations will come from trust and empowerment.

The following table illustrates the way workplace priorities have changed over time.

OLD		NEW
formal communication		abbreviations & emoticons
emails		collaborative technologies
formal learning style		virtual learning style
knowledge focussed		adaptive learning focussed
advice from official sources		advice through forums & chatbots
commanding leader		collaborative leader

controlling leadership style		empowering leadership style
work in office 9-5		work anywhere any time
outcome driven		purpose driven
print marketing		digital & social marketing

Changes in workplace practices

©Jessica Schubert

One of the highest priorities for younger generations is ensuring purpose before profit. Many young people seek to join organisations that lead with mission and purpose, and have a corporate culture that reflects the same. They want to change the world while also pursuing self-improvement, and they want employers to help. They feel that classic workforce models, old workplace policies, and performance-management standards need to adapt to the times.

Traditionally, however, corporate culture has been top down and rigid, with mandated working hours, seating arrangements and lunch breaks; basically, the antithesis of the model the new generation of workers would like to see. Millennials and Generation Z are seeking workplaces where they can work anytime from anywhere, which suits the hybrid and flexible workplace of the 21st century.

Millennials and Generation Z are hyperconnected yet disengaged. Younger generations are asking for more feedback, collaboration and cross-departmental engagement. Organisations need to take advantage of digital technology to stay in touch with their workforces, but must also be smart about the output. The way younger generations work—their priorities, their value, their fears and motivators—is probably different from yours if you are Generation X or a baby boomer. Technology is just the enabler; conversations are key.

> ' WE NEED TO REMEMBER ACROSS
> GENERATIONS THAT THERE IS AS MUCH
> TO LEARN AS THERE IS TO TEACH.'
>
> —GLORIA STEINEM

Megatrend 2: Technological Progress

The megatrend that I call technological progress covers digitalisation, automation and artificial intelligence. These three categories represent different types of technological progress, but often go hand in hand in a change-management process. For example, one of my clients in the finance industry is in the process of automating HR processes, which will only be possible if all documents are digitalised at the same time.

> ' GETTING INFORMATION OFF THE
> INTERNET IS LIKE TAKING A DRINK FROM
> A FIRE HOSE.'
>
> —MITCHELL KAPOR

Technological progress is the one megatrend that not only has the greatest impact on businesses around the world, but its implementation should also be a priority for many organisations in order to manage risk and stay competitive.

We are in the midst of a technological revolution that is changing the way we live and work. There are many unknowns, the change is fast and complex, and no one can really know how it will all unfold. Which brings me back to VUCA. An article by the World Economic Forum describes the term 'Fourth Industrial Revolution' like this: 'When compared with previous industrial revolutions, the Fourth is evolving at an exponential rather than a linear pace. Moreover, it is disrupting almost every industry in every country.

And the breadth and depth of these changes herald the transformation of entire systems of production, management, and governance.'[3]

Technological progress impacts the way we look at our products and services, and how we can improve them for consumers. Every day new digital platforms pop up, offering services that make our processes and lives easier. It's no longer about catching up with technology; it's about *embracing* technology and being at the forefront of innovation to stay competitive. With technological progress we also need to adapt our organisational models, look at how we structure our workplaces, and encourage our people to lead the future.

One of the 12 Skills needed to lead the future is the embrace of technology. I explain what that means for leaders and also share strategies in a later chapter.

Digitalisation

Digital transformation is the process of using digital technologies to create new, or modify existing, business processes, culture, and customer experiences to meet changing business and market requirements. There are some obvious trailblazers that are leading the digital game in the world. These companies have led the way in transforming customer experience through digital transformation.

Bitcoin	The world's biggest bank, with no actual cash.
Uber	The world's largest taxi company, owns no vehicles
Facebook	The world's most popular media owner, creates no content.
Alibaba	The world's most valuable retailer, has no inventory.
Airbnb	The world's largest accomodation provider, owns no real estate

Of course, many organisations use digital platforms, but they can't ignore the need for innovative digital transformation if they want to stay competitive. Leaders need to evaluate the ways in which digital platforms improve employee and customer experience. Since many people have been forced to work from home during lockdowns, we have seen a greater buy-in by organisations to connect their employees and clients digitally. Communication and social platforms have enabled millions of home-based people to stay connected, communicate and be productive in their jobs. This forced need to go digital can be achieved with great benefits.

> ‘FUTURE GENERATIONS WILL LOOK BACK ON TV AS THE LEAD IN THE WATER PIPES THAT SLOWLY DROVE THE ROMANS MAD.’
>
> —KURT VONNEGUT

For leaders all over the world, digital transformation is front and centre in the near future. In fact, a recent Deloitte survey states that for the ninety-four percent of interviewed CEOs globally, digitalisation is their priority for the next ten years.

I work with businesses in a wide range of industries, from travel to hospitality, retail to aviation, design to consulting, IT to banking. Digitalisation, with a focus on improving customer experience and internal processes, is part of everyone's remit, and the pressure to transform businesses has only become stronger since the Covid-19 pandemic forced us to change the way we work and deliver services.

I have experienced this firsthand. When all my face-to-face business was cancelled at the start of the pandemic, I had to learn to think on my feet. I knew that my clients still needed help with coaching and developing soft skills, especially now. There had always been a virtual element to my business because I worked with international clients, but now was my chance to digitalise my business on a larger scale. For me, it was all about transforming learning opportunities so they had the same impact as face-to-face interventions. I knew it wasn't possible to simply transfer to a virtual platform a workshop that was intended to cover a full day in a conference room.

I worked hard with my clients to redesign and run training and group-coaching sessions, using different online platforms with all their new functionalities to deliver impactful learning sessions. For me it's not just about using virtual platforms; it's about maximising the user experience specific to what my clients need from me. I also use different digital platforms for pre-recorded online learning courses that reach a wide audience, live webcasts, and e-book functionalities.

Having grown the business from a side hustle to an international leader in coaching and leadership development, I had to mainstream my internal processes, and with the help of my wonderful team we now run a paperless business that is interconnected using the most effective digital platforms. It's an ever-evolving venture, with new services being offered every week. It's a priority for my team and myself to stay on top of it, and we continue to transform the business for our clients.

Digital transformation can also have a negative impact, and when it does it's usually the human individual that suffers. Many of us are hyperconnected every minute of the day and are glued to our smartphones. I sometimes fear that we are losing focus on what's really important, namely, human connection, deep conversations, and time to reflect. I also see the negative impact of digital connectedness in the workplace. Employees tell me that they feel they are always *on*, receiving a constant flood of emails and instant messages.

Online conferencing platforms have been a huge blessing in the last few months. They have enabled many of us to continue working and running businesses from home, but bad habits and lack of boundaries can result in people feeling burnt out. It's a slippery slope. As leaders, we need to look after our people's health and wellbeing. Digital transformation can't be enabler and destroyer at the same time; leaders and organisations must maximise the use of digital platforms, while at the time minimising the human cost.

Artificial intelligence

Artificial intelligence (AI) represents great opportunities, but it's also perceived as a threat to the knowledge worker of the 21st century. There's an ongoing fear that machines will take people's jobs, but it's important to remember that while AI capabilities will be able to automate large amounts of manual processes, it will also create new job opportunities.

'ARTIFICIAL INTELLIGENCE IS THE NEW ELECTRICITY.'

—ANDREW NG

In a September 2020 article in the *Harvard Business Review*, Alex Kantrowitz explains how Amazon automated large parts of their processes under a program called 'hands off the wheel'. The program's goal was to automate processes by implementing machine learning, while at the same time reassigning workers to other tasks in the organisation.

In less than ten years Amazon's retail division has automated eighty percent of the company's processes. With enough data and learning predictions, their system was able to make its own decisions. Instead of letting the affected workers go, Amazon moved a large number of people from the retail division into product and program-manager jobs, where they are now part of innovation, helping the business grow in other departments.[4]

Data, being the lifeblood of artificial intelligence as it extracts meaning from it, has become one of the most valuable resources of the 21st century. Without growing volumes and speed of data, we are also seeing an evolution of AI. Artificial intelligence can be described as human intelligence exhibited by machines, or supervised learning where technology is able to perform specific tasks as well as, or better than, humans.

We program and code machines to do specific tasks. Face-recognition technology is a good example of what is called 'narrow AI'. In the 1990s, machine learning came to a rise, where machines were able to use algorithms to parse data, learn from it, and make predictions about the future without having to be programmed to do so.

The newest AI technology—deep learning—started in the mid-2010s. This learning is based on deep neural networks. The artificial neural networks have discrete layers, connections and directions of data propagation. For some, a picture of dystopian science fiction might come to mind, but AI and its evolution in learning capabilities offers great opportunities, which we can see already in technologies like driverless cars and preventive healthcare.

The greatest fear of employees around the world is not robots taking over the world but machines taking over human jobs. Global consulting firm McKinsey predicts that in about sixty percent of occupations, at least one-third of activities can be automated, meaning workers will be displaced. New jobs are being created at speed, and new skills need to be developed, creating even more opportunities. It's the responsibility of schools and universities to embrace new technology and teach relevant skills and capabilities.

Sixty-five percent of the children who are in middle school right now will be in jobs that don't yet exist when they become adults. These numbers might change over the next decade as governance and implementation play a big part in realising automation and AI, but the statistics and existing data are good indicators of where we are headed.[5]

What this means for businesses is that they will need to evaluate the opportunities that automation and AI offer them and their clients, and decide if AI is needed to stay competitive in their market. Hand in hand with automation processes, businesses need to review their workforce strategies, and implement relevant training and development to set up their employees and businesses for success in the work-world future.

Leaders need to be open to learning new skills and opportunities that technological progress offers, and refocus on human-to-human interactions. Humans will not be replaced, and leaders need to have a refreshed view on workplace structures, capabilities and what it takes to lead the future together.

Megatrend 3: The Future of Work

This might be the most talked-about megatrend right now. Over the next decade there will be many changes to the way work is carried out, who does it, and where it is done. So far in this book I have covered changes in the way work will be done by showing the effects of digitalisation, automation and AI. In this section I will talk about where this work will be done, and how remote and hybrid work models are impacting individuals, teams and organisations.

> 'ONE DAY OFFICES WILL BE A THING OF THE PAST.'
> —SIR RICHARD BRANSON

Remote and hybrid work models

Imagine yourself staying in bed an extra forty-five minutes on a Monday morning because you have no commute. At nine am in your home office, you flip open your laptop, coffee in hand, and work through your emails, attend Monday online team meetings, and finish a report in the afternoon before heading out for a run.

On Tuesday you commute to the city office, working with your project team on a client solution for most of the day. You spend Wednesday and Thursday on site with a client, and on Friday you decide to spend the morning doing some focused work at home before heading into the office in the afternoon to finish off the week in one-to-one meetings with some of your team members. At five pm it's time to socialise for after-work drinks with colleagues you haven't seen for a while.

Does that sound sweet to you? Or does it sound like your worst nightmare? Either way, it represents a work model most organisations are considering in the middle of 2021 as vaccination is underway all over the world and employees are starting to return to the office.

Remote working as such is neither a new term nor a new way of working, but it has been the main mode of working since whole workforces have been made to work from home throughout the Covid-19 pandemic. It has been an astonishing effort in a battle to combat a deadly disease, keeping workers safe and businesses running.

There was a widespread view that employees wouldn't go back to the old nine-to-five office setup, and instead a new-normal and now next-normal work structure has been created. Organisations that hadn't already bought into remote work realised that their businesses continued without a hitch when people were forced to work from home, and they saw real advantages in having distributed teams. Employees quickly adapted to making the dining room their office, appreciating the lack of commute time and being able to spend more time with their families or their hobbies.

What exactly is remote and hybrid working? Remote work means employees work from anywhere, often without a central physical office. In this case, employees work from home, on site with clients, or even at their holiday homes or in a hotel. In hybrid-work models, employees work from the office some days and remotely on others. Individual organisations have been busy figuring out the most suitable model for them by considering job types, client needs, organisational goals, and culture and employee preference. Here are the most popular models being considered:

- Full time in the office: all employees are asked to work in the office all of the time
- Full time at home: no central office exists, and everyone works from home all of the time
- Remote hybrid: the office is still there when it's needed, but attendance is optional
- Flexible hybrid: employees can work from home, but still use the office for teamwork, and travel to clients' premises
- Planned hybrid: a 2:3 or 3:2 ratio, either working from home or in the office
- Tiered hybrid: depending on the type of work, certain workers come back to the office full time or have flexibility to choose a 2:3-ratio structure

Some organisations choose the full-time office option while others opt for the full-time remote structure. The most popular option is a hybrid model, where employees split their time between working from home and working in the office. In fact, a recent PricewaterhouseCoopers survey shows that eighty-three percent of business leaders say remote work has been successful for their company, but only thirteen percent say that they're ready to let go of the office for good. The overwhelming majority say the office is important for collaborating with team members and building relationships.[6]

Hybrid models come with myriad benefits for both organisations and employees, but they also create challenges for workers and leaders, who have to decide how to make everything work well for everyone. Let's look at some of the challenges around leadership and the actual workspace, and the issues that organisations need to consider when designing new office space.

The office-space challenge

Organisations all across the world are downsizing and reconfiguring their office space. This means not only substantial cost savings for companies and a reduction in their carbon footprint, but it also offers a unique opportunity to design a workspace that supports a particular work culture *and* enables productivity.

'A HYBRID NATURE OF ORGANISATION STRIKES THE RIGHT BALANCE BETWEEN "VIRTUAL WORLD" AND THE HUMAN CONNECTIONS.'

—PERAL ZHU

I am currently working with a client in the technology industry here in Melbourne. After making their entire company work from home, they struggled when it came time for people to return to the office in the CBD. Some employees had relocated to the countryside or seaside, not expecting to have to come back to the physical office space.

I sat down with the managing director, let's call him Wayne, to discuss the challenges and possible opportunities involved with creating the next normal for his workforce. Generally speaking, people don't want to come back to the office; they don't miss the commute, and they don't miss being in that physical space. What they do miss, however, is the connection with other people, along with a sense of contributing to the purpose of the organisation.

Wayne realised that it was time to involve his team in deciding what the new office space and work models would look like. He interviewed over two hundred employees from all levels and departments of the organisation, following which he set up round-table meetings and diverse project groups with the aim of coming up with a plan.

As a result, the organisation now has a much smaller central office that is designed for teams to come together and collaborate, meet clients and socialise. Wayne has also agreed to open satellite offices around Australia, using co-working spaces. This means employees can avoid long commutes while still being able to work from an office when they need to. The central office is designed to foster innovation and collaboration, and every piece of furniture, artwork and technical device plays its part in making the environment fun and effective. The happy outcome is that employees now want to come to the office.

I realise this is a very specific example, but I encourage you to think about the purpose that would be the driver in your own work culture. Global consulting firm McKinsey has developed the following framework, which puts purpose, value and culture at the centre of any post-pandemic organisation.[7]

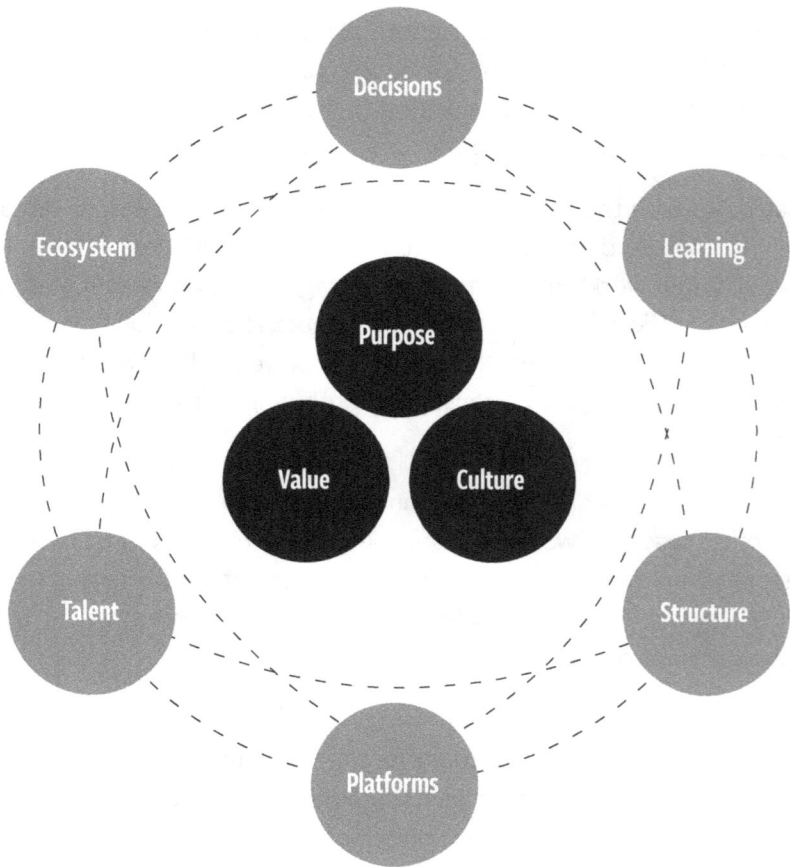

McKinsey's purpose, value and culture model. Source: McKinsey

In the article titled 'Reimagining the Postpandemic Organization', the author advises: 'Get specific and take action on building a culture that fosters employee engagement, both in-office and remote.'

Also consider these aspects when designing the space:

- Create meeting spaces for a hybrid work model, employing different-sized conference rooms equipped with high-quality video cameras, large screens, microphones and speakers to provide accurate and seamless technical experiences for those taking meetings in and out of the office.
- Eliminate technical issues and invest in your infrastructure. This will enhance the quality of experience for all employees, both those in the space and remote workers. Remote workers should feel included, even when they're not in the workspace.
- Utilise workspaces that are well designed for project work and collaboration, with fit-for-purpose furniture and magnetic whiteboards.
- Have movable desks and standing desks, with state-of-the-art connectivity and configurations. Such quiet zones and study booths enable focused work and productivity.
- Instead of archaic tearooms, design social hubs that foster interaction and people want to hang out. Check out WeWork spaces for modern and practical designs.
- Before ordering furniture and a new coffee machine, have a clear understanding of how and why you want your workforce to use the space. A failure to design workspaces with your people and culture in mind drives the risk of spaces not being used at all.

Work arrangements in a hybrid world

Planned hybrid is the option most of the leaders I work with are considering right now. They want their people to spend some time in the office for crucial face-to-face interactions, such as complex problem-solving, collaborating and innovating, but they also want to offer flexibility to work from home on some days.

'TECHNOLOGY NOW ALLOWS PEOPLE TO CONNECT ANYTIME, ANYWHERE, TO ANYONE IN THE WORLD, FROM ALMOST ANY DEVICE. THIS IS DRAMATICALLY CHANGING THE WAY PEOPLE WORK, FACILITATING 24/7 COLLABORATION WITH COLLEAGUES WHO ARE DISPERSED ACROSS TIME ZONES, COUNTRIES AND CONTINENTS.'

—MICHAEL DELL

On the next page is a helpful model for keeping productivity in mind. Lynda Gratton presented this work-arrangement model in a recent *Harvard Business Review* article as a way of deciding which work arrangement works best, depending on the nature of the job.[8]

Think about the tasks performed by your individual employees and consider critical drivers of productivity for each, e.g. energy, focus, coordination, corporation. Determine which work arrangement is most suitable for them and how it will impact the drivers if it changes.

For example, a team manager's driver of productivity is coordination. A team manager needs to coordinate work, give updates and feedback, and help problem-solve in the moment so team members can continue to work. Time has to be asynchronous, but it's not necessary to work in the same space; work can be done anywhere during the day, from nine to five.

For solution architects and innovators, cooperation would be the main driver, and face-to-face time would be critical for productivity. The main office space or, even better, innovation hub and satellite offices, would be most suitable for this type of work.

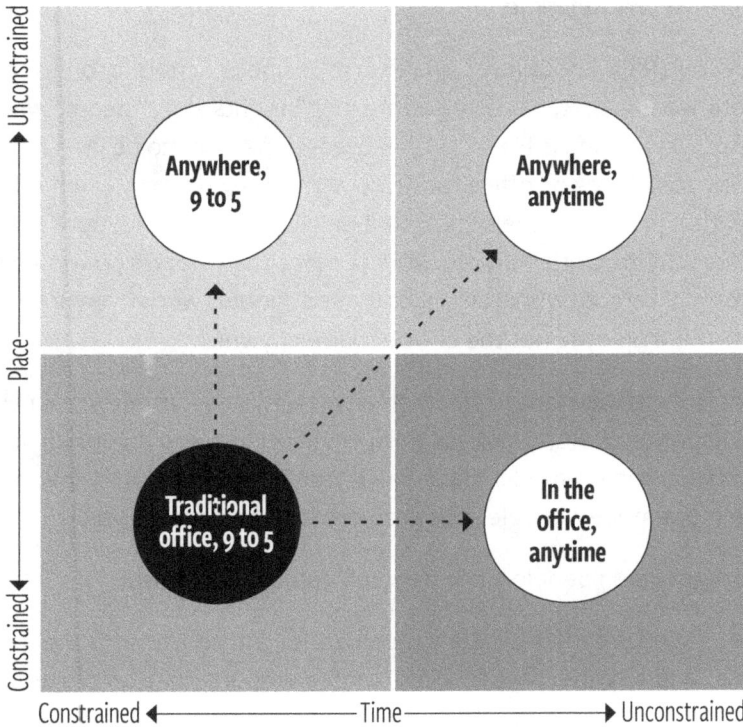

Lynda Gratton's work-arrangement model. Source: Harvard Business Review

Data analysts are most productive when they can focus, and the anywhere-anytime arrangement works best for them because their work doesn't depend on others. They can also decide if they prefer to work from home or in the office, or even split a day between the two.

Lynda Gratton's model offers a great way to plan the way forward with your workforce, focusing on drivers of productivity but also considering personal preferences. Everyone's personal situation is different, and as leaders and employers we must consider all circumstances.

Work anywhere, anytime

Prithwiraj (Raj) Choudhury, a Harvard Business School professor and remote-work expert, has some interesting insights about people wanting to return to the office. He says: 'Employees don't "long to be in the office", or miss commutes or office furniture. What they do miss when it is not recreated remotely is the same communication and connections that are fundamental to work. Remote work is more than work-from-home, and the form of remote work I am most excited about is work-from-anywhere, where the employee has the choice to live anywhere.'

Most organisations want to give their employees freedom while maintaining productivity and organisational performance, so some form of hybrid is the most common model that's being tested right now. And that means there is a remote-work element that needs to be considered.

Challenges when people work remotely (part or full time):

- Sense of inequality: It's much easier for people with big houses and a spare room to work comfortably at home. Employees who live in shared accommodation or small city apartments struggle to work effectively when the dining table is their permanent desk.
- Magnification of the gender gap: Women are disproportionally expected to take on home-based caring responsibilities, making working from home more challenging.
- Lack of fairness: There are different rules for different people. Parents with school children are perceived to have preferential status compared to single people without dependants.
- Different personalities are not considered: Some people need routine, which can be difficult to find at home, while others thrive when there is constant change. No size fits all.
- Social disconnect: There can be a lack of visibility and exchange, and disparities are inevitable. There is a danger of creating silos, which can lead to knowledge loss.
- Innovation slowdown: Workshopping, innovating and complex-solving are much harder when using digital platforms. If not

facilitated well, there could be a loss of creativity and collective wisdom.

- Out of sight, out of mind: Employees have less access to resources, mentors, coffee chats, or even just opportunities to bump into stakeholders and decision makers. In a remote-work environment, employees have a real fear around lack of opportunities for career progression.

As a leader, there are many things to consider. There's no perfect solution and it's an evolving piece, but one thing is clear: most organisations won't go back to the way things were. Some additional points to consider:

- Be intentional with your plan forward, and have clarity about what kind of work culture you want in your team or organisation.
- Use Lynda Gratton's work-arrangement model as a guideline for your senior executives and line managers so they can agree on a structure that works best for high productivity as well as personal preference.
- Be effective and fair when it comes to making things work for the organisation as well as the individual. Having empathy and an understanding of someone's personal situation and needs while setting expectations and asking for accountability is key.
- Have a high level of clarity and consistency around procedures and processes, especially when they change. Transparent communication, clear guidelines and relevant technology set you up for success.
- Move to output-centric work cultures. Reward results rather than hours in the office, otherwise it will be impossible to lead your people and measure success. This will take some time, but you have to make it a priority for all team leaders to adopt.
- Keep in mind that people must be safe and healthy. You have a duty of care towards your remote employees, who must be able to stay safe and healthy. Have safety moments in meetings, train your leaders to have tough conversations, be supportive, and offer practical wellness opportunities for all employees.

- Create a culture of empowerment and trust that is assimilated in a hybrid world. This is probably the most important part of getting hybrid right. In a recent study by talent mobility platform Topia, the majority of respondents stated that empowerment and trust were the most important factors for a 'great employee experience', compared with the sixteen percent who saw a 'cool looking' office space as a priority.

Remember, you get hybrid right if you keep the human in mind.

Megatrend 4: Globalisation

The world is getting smaller. According to Barack Obama, 'Globalisation is a fact, because of technology, because of an integrated supply chain, because of changes in transportation. And we're not going to be able to build a wall around that.'

The term *globalisation* describes the way countries and people around the world interact and integrate. It's the process by which businesses or other organisations develop international influence or start operating on an international scale. It's a broad term covering the way that people, businesses, governments and economies interconnect in the world. The scale of globalisation can be increased through speed, means of communication and connectedness, but it can also be disrupted by events like the 2008 global financial crisis, Brexit, and the large-scale tariffs imposed during the Trump administration.

The world was holding its breath as the pandemic first began to sweep the world, in fear that border closures, and a halt on most international travel and trade could have a lasting negative impact on globalisation. There was a significant dip in cross-border flows in 2020, but data from 2021 shows a bright future for growing globalisation. The landscape of the way we work has changed as a result of the remote-work megatrend, and businesses and leaders are being faced with new challenges; however, they are also being offered great opportunities to reorganise their workplaces and human resources strategies.

In a 2021 *Harvard Business Review* article, authors Steven A Altman and Phillip Bastian shared the implications for the four segments of cross-border flows by which globalisation is measured. Data shows that in the first few months of 2021, trade flow had rebounded strongly, capital flows were recovering, and digital information flows had surged. The only segment impacted negatively by Covid-19 had been people flow.[9]

In 2020 the number of people travelling internationally fell by seventy-four percent, and a recovery to pre-pandemic levels is not expected until at least 2023. Business travel has changed for good as organisations have realised that a high number of business meetings and interactions work just as efficiently using digital platforms.

Many industries have been left devastated in the wake of the global pandemic, especially aviation and tourism, whereas other industries have flourished. Online conferencing platforms like Zoom and e-commerce platforms all around the world have benefited from the way people have changed their communication and consumer behaviour. International internet traffic has soared, and so has cross-border e-commerce.

Organisations have been taking advantage of globalised human resources structures for some time and it's on the rise in Asia in particular. Call centres and manufacturing, for example, have been outsourced to Southeast Asia for years. Entire workforces have been made to work from home for long periods of time during the pandemic, and organisations have realised that remote work, when done well, not only saves costs but also widens the talent pool.

I am currently working with a client in the finance industry in Melbourne who has been embracing the hybrid work model, giving employees the flexibility to decide whether to work from home or in the office. Not only does this enable existing team members to live wherever they like without having to consider the daily commute, but it also allows the organisation to change their hiring strategy. In the last six months, the company has hired several interstate employees, and even a few people located in India and the Philippines. The organisation is now able to hire on merit and for best fit rather than geography.

'REALISE THAT HIRING A MORE DIVERSE TEAM WILL GIVE YOU A WHOLE NEW REPERTOIRE OF INNOVATIVE IDEAS.'

—DAVID LIVERMORE

Besides the obvious fact of widening the talent pool, there are several other added benefits to having teams with multicultural layers:

- People bring different viewpoints; they not only see the world from a different angle, but also have experience working or living in different cultures that might be key to understanding global clientele.
- People bring different approaches to problem-solving, decision-making and creativity.
- Each person has to flex their empathy muscle, which leads to a more cohesive team culture.

With increased flexibility comes greater opportunity to attract top talent, but it also comes with the responsibility of leading these more diverse teams. Organisations must equip their leaders with the right skills to lead multicultural teams. Leaders don't just facilitate collaboration between people with different backgrounds; they forge new team spirit, and they mould cultures where everyone respects one another, and they use their strengths and emotional intelligence to work together.

What we as leaders have realised during the pandemic and the move to a more globalised workforce is that the focus has to be on developing our people. Leading virtual and cross-cultural teams requires new skills, and as leaders we have to make sure we set up our people for success. Leading remote teams is one of the 12 Skills I cover in this book, and I share strategies and tools in a later chapter.

Megatrend 5: Environment

Coral reefs are dying due to rising water temperatures, raging wildfires caused by ongoing droughts are destroying thousands of hectares of land and killing billions of animals, oceans are being overfished, and large-scale animal farms, manufacturing plants and an increasing number of cars and trucks on the road mean CO_2 levels are skyrocketing to dangerous levels. Environmental disasters are the biggest and most imminent threat to humanity, and there is increasing evidence that our planet is in crisis.

> THE ENVIRONMENT AND THE ECONOMY ARE REALLY BOTH TWO SIDES OF THE SAME COIN. IF WE CANNOT SUSTAIN THE ENVIRONMENT, WE CANNOT SUSTAIN OURSELVES.'
>
> —WANGARI MAATHAI

If politicians and businesses don't act, climate change could have a disastrous impact on world hunger, mass migration, and the collapse of global financial markets. Governments are struggling to commit to net zero emission plans, but at least these conversations are at the centre of global summits. Businesses around the world are reconsidering their purpose, and according to a Deloitte Global Readiness Report, six out of ten global companies surveyed claim they have internal sustainability plans in place.

Millennials and Generation Z, born in 1980 and earlier, want to see a change in the way sustainability is adopted by businesses. For younger generations, it's not good enough to have a blurb about sustainability on a company's website; they're demanding action and commitment. As I explained in Megatrend 1: Demographics and Multigenerations, Millennials and Generation Z have a purpose-before-profit mindset, and businesses are reacting. Organisations are switching to renewable resources for electricity, recycling is being encouraged in almost every corporate office, and product designers and innovators are being tasked to use more environmentally friendly materials.

A *Forbes* article written in 2020 states: 'More and more, the pursuit of similar actions to reduce environmental impact and benefit society will be necessary for businesses to survive, let alone thrive. Consumers are demanding that the companies they patronise do more to be good corporate citizens. They're speaking with their voices and their wallets, and they're not inclined to take "no" for an answer. Fortunately, profit incentives—as well as executives' increasing fears about climate change's potential negative effect on business operations—are giving companies plenty of reasons to join with citizens and act on climate change.'[10]

IMPACT ON WORKPLACES AND LEADERSHIP

I hope by now you have gained some insight into the global drivers of change. I now want to connect the dots and explain how leadership is impacted as a result of megatrends, with a focus on today's reality.

My workload has doubled, but my hours haven't. This is a comment I hear all too often from employees these days. People all over the world have shown great amounts of adaptability and flexibility during the pandemic, in particular over the first few months of 2021. They have made their home their temporary office space, home-schooled their children, and adapted to using virtual tools to stay connected.

MEGATRENDS: COMPLEXITY, PACE, CONNECTIVITY

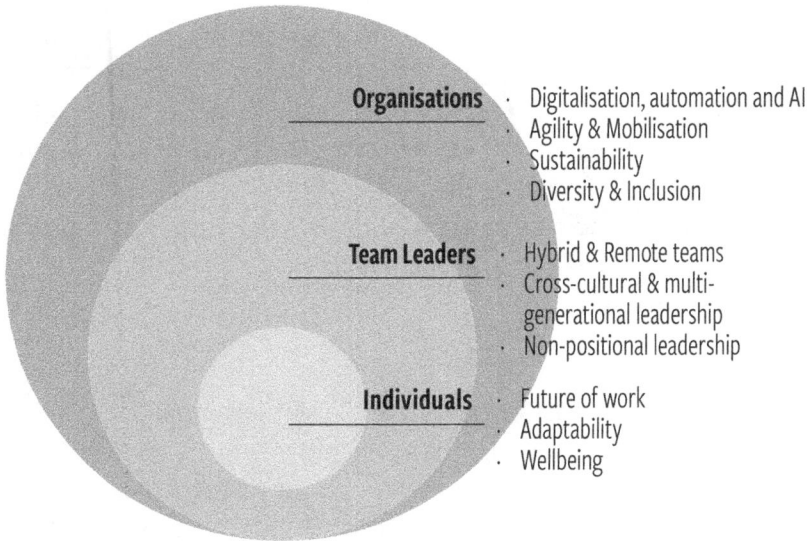

Organisations
- Digitalisation, automation and AI
- Agility & Mobilisation
- Sustainability
- Diversity & Inclusion

Team Leaders
- Hybrid & Remote teams
- Cross-cultural & multi-generational leadership
- Non-positional leadership

Individuals
- Future of work
- Adaptability
- Wellbeing

Individuals, team leaders and organisations are impacted differently, but all have complexity, pace and connectivity in common.

When the world went into its first lockdowns, the greatest fear leaders had was of a decrease in productivity. In fact, it has been the opposite for most organisations. People have shown that they can be more productive working, at least part time, from home. Productivity seems to go up, but at what cost?

Due to general uncertainty in particular markets, organisations are hesitant about increasing their workforces, and even the replacement of exiting employees has stalled. Almost every client I work with has undergone a number of restructures in their organisations since the pandemic began, and the general feedback is that there is a lot of change, more work, more responsibility and fewer resources. Companies are bracing themselves for what they perceive as a volatile economy ahead and employees are paying for it.

While most companies state that the change to more remote work has been successful, there are obvious challenges in the way employees collaborate and communicate. In a physical workspace we can see how much work individuals are doing at any time, for instance, when they are in meetings, when they are at their desks, and when they are with clients. Without that transparency, many leaders' demands for delivery of work have increased, expected timeframes have become tighter, and everyone thinks every email has to lead to a conference call. False urgency and constant availability are testing people, putting some individuals at the brink of their capacity.

The urgency trap

Everyone is in such a rush these days. We quickly move from one meeting to another, speed-read through emails, and reply in a similar reactive fashion in order to squeeze in as many pieces of communication as possible before the end of the working day, only to run out the door for school pick-up, football drop-off and other social activities. Everything is urgent, and everything is done in a rush. It is exhausting.

In our personal and business lives, urgency has massively increased in the last two decades. Technology has enabled us to communicate faster and easier across different geographical regions. Remember how exciting it was in the 1990s with the introduction of email? We were all so sure that emails would save us time. And when most of us shifted to online platforms during 2020 we realised that we didn't even have to be in the same physical space to meet with our teams, we just had to use Microsoft Teams and Slack.

But when I speak to leaders now, they tell me they're exhausted and burnt out. Everyone feels like they're simply reacting to emails, instant messages and online chats, and they don't have the time to slow down, think and create. Every task seems more urgent than the last.

A friend of mine who works for a large PR firm recently described her day to me as a long string of online meetings with clients and peers with hardly a break. Her time for creating concepts starts at six pm, but of course by that time she's tired and has little creative brain capacity left to do the real work. 'Why has everything become so urgent?' she said to me. 'I feel like I'm constantly putting out fires and everyone needs an answer from me that simply cannot seem to wait.'

You can see that working in this way, in a haze of deadlines and last-minute meetings, is neither sustainable nor productive. I'm not saying that we shouldn't have any urgency. In fact, urgency helps us deliver projects on time, and it creates friction that is sometimes necessary for our teams and ourselves to move forward. It's not about ignoring the need for urgency; it's about finding the right kind of urgency that will help us be more productive.

In his book *Urgent*, Dermot Crowley describes three zones in which we operate: reactive, active and inactive. In the reactive zone we experience acute urgency. If it doesn't happen too often it can be helpful in creating traction and momentum, but if we stay in this zone too long, as my friend at the PR firm does, it turns into what Crowley calls 'acute and chronic urgency', which results in stress and burnout.

Virtual-meeting madness

Do you feel exhausted just looking at your daily calendar packed with Zoom or team meetings? Does it feel like pulling teeth getting your team to engage and come up with ideas in online workshops? Are you experiencing a sense of disconnect with some team members when you're chatting with them in the conference room while others are 'zoomed in' remotely?

This is the new reality for most leaders and teams. Communicating virtually is and will be a large part of our daily lives for the foreseeable future. In this new mode of working, people have had to learn how to use virtual platforms effectively, reprioritise tasks throughout the day, manage their energy to avoid Zoom fatigue, and influence stakeholders. Zoom fatigue is very real. Recent Stanford research has identified four causes of fatigue during video chats:[11]

- Excessive amount of highly intense, close eye contact
- Fatigue at seeing ourselves constantly in real time
- Reduction of our usual mobility
- Higher cognitive load

Working with leaders all around the world, I have witnessed what I call 'virtual-meeting madness'. This is what it looks like:

- Too many virtual meetings: every email now seems to lead to a virtual meeting
- Virtual meetings are too long: there's no need for every meeting to last for one hour
- Too many people in meetings: just because it's easy to link people in it doesn't mean they have to be there
- Meetings without a clear purpose: these are often standing weekly team meetings, or meetings that are helpful for the leader but no one else
- Meetings with no clear agenda: attendees are not sure what is expected, conversations don't hit the point, meetings run over
- Monopolisation by the same team members: the same few team members bring themselves in, which means lack of consistent input from the whole team, and this results in disengagement

I coach dozens of teams where I have the privilege of being part of their meetings. What I see time and time again is a mix of all of the above meeting-madness behaviours:

- Too much time involved in team members giving department updates and sharing complex data
- Leaders monopolising the majority of the airtime
- People talking over each other
- The same team members not bringing themselves in, and quite obviously working on other things on their phones during the meetings

I see too many meetings that are ineffective, inefficient and unproductive. And if that frustrates me, imagine how it is for your team members, who possibly have several of these meetings each week. The effects we are seeing include employees working longer hours to 'catch up on real work', becoming more disengaged during virtual meetings, multitasking, and being physically and mentally exhausted after spending too much time online.

To keep people engaged, healthy, happy *and* productive means being more mindful when it comes to shaping the hybrid world of virtual work.

The big disconnect

We have never been more digitally connected and socially disconnected at the same time than we are right now. Connectivity has been one of the greatest accelerators of change in globalising the world in the last decade. Technological progress has enabled us to connect with anyone, anytime as long as we have a digital device and an internet connection. Social media platforms are a wonderful way for us to stay in touch with our friends and update them on our day-to-day lives. To find your next date you don't even have to go to the pub anymore; you just swipe right.

Technological progress and digital connectivity can push people into loneliness and eliminate what is really important: human connection, conversations and intimacy. We're all familiar with images of people sitting in cafes together, each person staring separately at their own device.

Human connection is just as important in the workplace as in our personal lives, and with the increase in numbers of people working according to remote and hybrid models, human interactions have decreased. A 2017 *Harvard Business Review* survey showed that over half the people who worked remotely felt that they were not treated equally. These people claimed to feel left out and isolated, and afraid of what was being said behind their backs. In the shift towards even more remote work since the pandemic, this problem has only increased. There is a real danger of people feeling lonely and unsupported.

My advice is to disconnect (from your device) to reconnect (with humans).

The shallow-work problem

Being connected through email, Microsoft Teams, Slack channels and Instant Messenger, just to name a few channels, helps us communicate effectively with clients and other team members, and state-of-the-art software ensures that we stay productive. Or so we think.

There's no denying that technology has enabled us to deliver work faster and accelerate business transactions. I remember printing out proposals and sending them to prospective clients via traditional mail in the early 1990s, which seems unthinkable now in terms of manual effort and speed of sales conversion. Then came email, and like everyone else I thought it was going to save me so much time. If only.

How are you?

I'm good, but so busy.

This is the start of pretty much every conversation I have these days.

No matter which industry they work in, everyone is telling me how busy they are. Long workdays merging into work on weekends, endless to-do lists, hundreds of emails a day, and back-to-back Zoom meetings ... Everyone is crazy busy. Yet when we address team or organisational challenges we're encountering a lack of productivity and not the state of busyness everyone claims to be in.

When tackling productivity with my clients (or the lack thereof), I have noticed two things: they're spending too much time on shallow work, and they're not spending enough time on deep work.

Most people spend over seventy percent of their time replying to emails and messages, managing their diaries and CRM, completing reports, and doing various administrative tasks for client or team management. Only about thirty percent of time is spent on creation, innovation or complex problem-solving. That seventy percent of time is spent doing shallow work. According to Cal Newport, author of *Deep Work*, shallow work is 'non-cognitively demanding, logistical style tasks, often performed while

---

distracted. The efforts tend to not create much value in the world and are easy to replicate'.

We often make shallow work our priority, doing it first thing in the morning, and we tend to go back to doing shallow work because we consider it easy. Yet these are the exact tasks that make us busy, distract us, and hold us back from being productive. Technology only enables us to be more productive if we use it in a productive way. If it leads us to focus on shallow work most of the time, it only increases our busyness.

How much empathy is too much empathy?

Many leaders have told me that applying empathy at work has been their main focus over the last eighteen months. But they also tell me that they feel drained by taking on the emotional burdens their people are going through in this still uncertain and ambiguous world. Conversations around regulating empathy in order to protect leaders from burnout are part of almost every coaching session I currently have with leaders and intact teams.

This year I worked with a senior leader who led his department through a major restructure due to the fallout of Covid-19, and he had to make dozens of people redundant. He put all of his energy into the process and conversations to make it as easy as possible for the people affected, and dialled up his empathy like never before. He was proud of how he had helped his people through the transition, but he came close to burnout in the process.

Another leader I coached shifted her entire workforce to working from home, created flexibility for a hybrid setup, increased one-on-one conversations and check-ins, and was always available to listen to what was going on for her people personally. She told me that although her team was appreciative, she didn't know how long she could stay strong for everyone.

These are just two of many similar stories. What these leaders have gone through is called 'empathy burnout', also described as being overwhelmed and exhausted by taking on too many negative emotions from others. I will be diving into the skill of building resilience and how to lead with empathy without burning out in a later chapter.

The world of work today has changed so much in the last decade as a result of being impacted by megatrends, which has only accelerated during the pandemic. I hope this comprehensive summary of the challenges involved will help you identify some of the issues you and your team might be struggling with. The 12 Skills in the last third of this book will build on that by giving you steps, models and strategies for leading the future.

'THE BEST WAY TO PREDICT THE FUTURE IS TO CREATE IT.'

—ABRAHAM LINCOLN

CHAPTER 2

WHERE ARE YOU ON THE JOURNEY TO LEAD THE FUTURE?

I was born and raised in Germany, but I haven't lived there permanently since 2001. I grew up in the countryside just east of the city of Cologne with my older sister, mum and dad. My sister and I lost our father when I was eight years old, which was one of the most tragic and pivotal moments of my life. I had to learn to be independent, strong and self-sufficient very quickly when my mother went back into the workforce full time. I was a typical eighties kid, with the house key on a self-made string around my neck, spending the afternoons doing homework by myself and riding my pushbike to handball practice.

I have always been confident and optimistic, even as a child, so being independent and learning new skills, such as cooking and putting on a load of washing at the age of ten, wasn't hard for me. If anything, it made me even more independent, with a strong will to follow my own path and have big and bold goals.

No one was surprised about my decision to leave the safety of my home after high school to live and work in Australia for a year. No one apart from my mum, that is; she only believed it when I actually booked the ticket. I managed to get an office internship at my mum's partner's firm, which has a subsidiary on the outskirts of Melbourne.

It didn't really kick in for me that I was going to live twenty-five thousand kilometres away with people I had never met in a country I had never visited before, speaking a foreign language I had only learned in school—until I got on the plane by myself. I stopped crying on the stopover in Bangkok, brushed myself off and made friends on the last leg of my journey.

That year in Australia at the age of eighteen was one of the best learning experiences of my life. I learned to embrace a new culture, experienced the frustration of reaching my limit with a new language, and adjusted to being far away from family and friends. This was in the early nineties, so overseas communication was only possible by phone or fax.

Not only did I fall in love with the country that I have since made my home, but the experience of living abroad, with all its ups and downs, also made it easy for me to repeat that experience over and over again.

In 2001, back in Germany, I decided to take a year off from my corporate job in commercial real estate. I quit my job, stored all my furniture in my mum's attic and left Germany with a backpack and my Lonely Planet guidebook to discover the east coast of Australia. Although other people have helped me on this journey, I have made my dream a reality. I guess I've always had a knack for influencing people to get what I want.

I never made it back to Germany after that, not to live permanently anyway. I moved to New Zealand and lived there for three years, then lived and worked in Sydney and Melbourne before accepting an exciting and challenging job in Hong Kong in 2010; this in turn led to me living in Tokyo for six months.

I now live in Melbourne, running my own leadership practice. I wrote this book during Australia's fourth lockdown, brought about by Covid-19.

What I have learned throughout my journey so far is that life always changes. There are some things I don't have control over, for instance losing my dad, being exposed to workplace bullying at one of my jobs, or changing circumstances when the pandemic hit in early 2020. I have always seen challenges as opportunities, and this has helped me to adapt to change quickly, accept the things I can't change, and find a way forward.

I have worked and lived in many cities, countries and cultures, and that has given me the great advantage of creating awareness of who I am, strengths, challenges and all. When you are exposed to other cultures, you can look at your own culture from a distance and see more clearly the differences and commonalities. This skill has helped me immensely when leading diverse teams. I not only understand differences in skills and natural behaviour styles, but I'm also aware of how different cultural backgrounds impact team dynamics and relationships. I'm constantly learning new skills as my business evolves, adapting to new cultures through my work, responding to social markers like the Covid-19 pandemic and trying to predict what happens next.

My job is to help people identify what they're doing well and which areas they need to develop so they can be the leaders they want to be. My mission is to empower leaders to lead the future and mobilise the world.

FROM FOLLOWING TO LEADING THE FUTURE

The world is changing, and it's changing fast. Those of us who want to lead the future have to do it together; we can't do it alone. We need engaged teams and workforces to foresee change, create a vision of the future, and mobilise communities.

As leaders, we need to understand what our organisations and teams are most impacted by. The 5 Megatrends I described in the previous chapter are a great start, but I encourage everyone to identify factors that are most relevant to them specifically. We can't ignore outside factors and megatrends, nor can we expect to change them. What we can do is keep our employees engaged and equip them with the skills that matter right now; the skills they need to lead the future.

Team-member engagement has been identified as one of the most important drivers of business growth, and it is a strategy that has a direct impact on the performance of an organisation. But how can we measure team-member engagement?

After working with hundreds of leaders, I know that team members typically go through the 5 levels of engagement outlined in the following diagram before they're ready to lead the future.

TEAM-MEMBER ENGAGEMENT MODEL

	ACTIVITY	ENGAGEMENT	FOCUS	PERFORMANCE
5	Lead the future	Agile	Mobilise	100%
4	Lead change	Responsive	Co-create	75%
3	Lead others	Engaged	Integrate	50%
2	Lead self	Disengaged	Connect	25%
1	Following	Destructive	Self-awareness	0%

There are 5 levels of team-member engagement, each of which is measured by performance. Performance in this model doesn't just measure the achievement of organisational goals; it also takes into account how engaged the individual is, and how they feel they can achieve their potential and contribute to success.

- The activity column describes the behaviour observed on this level of team-member engagement, the type of interactions that occur between employees, the quality of conversations, leadership styles, and fear and motivation. This column helps you identify what level you or your team are on; it describes what is going on in your organisation.
- The engagement column describes the impact team-member engagement has on the individual, team and organisation.
- The focus column offers solutions: the next steps that you as a leader need to take to get to a higher level.
- The fourth column shows the level of performance you are most likely to see, and how much team member engagement increases by changing your focus at each level.

Engagement at the next level shows you that your effort is working. For example, when you create enough self-awareness for yourself and your team, you can then move from the destructive level to the disengaged level.

I have designed this model so you can easily gauge the level of team-member engagement in your organisation, how that impacts performance, and what to focus on to move up through the levels. I will now break it down even further and explore each of the 5 levels:

Level 1: Destructive

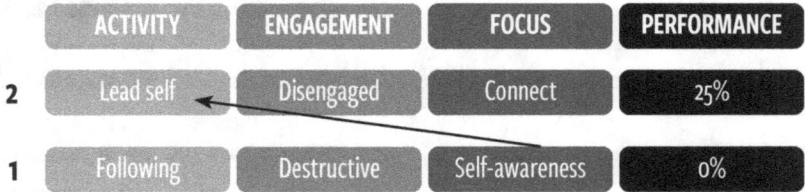

	ACTIVITY	ENGAGEMENT	FOCUS	PERFORMANCE
2	Lead self	Disengaged	Connect	25%
1	Following	Destructive	Self-awareness	0%

On level 1, the lowest level of team-member engagement, I describe the activity as 'following'. When I think of people working on this level, I picture lemmings, the northern European rodents that blindly follow each other to their death by running off cliffs. In fact, this is a widely held misconception. It's more probable that it is a migratory behaviour in large populations where the rodents could drown if the chosen body of water happened to be an ocean.

Employees on this level typically work for a pay cheque. They follow instructions without thinking too much about why they do what they do. Work doesn't feel meaningful for them, and even you as a team leader on this level might find yourself not believing in the purpose of the company and simply following the herd.

I describe the team-member engagement on this level as 'destructive'. Generally, the behaviour can make for a negative, or even toxic, culture. There is little social interaction, and what there is can often be dominated by gossip rather than personal, supportive conversations. In this kind of work environment, psychological safety is low so people generally have their guard up, which leads to a lack of meaningful contribution in team meetings. I find that the general leadership style here takes a command-and-control approach, often coupled with micromanagement.

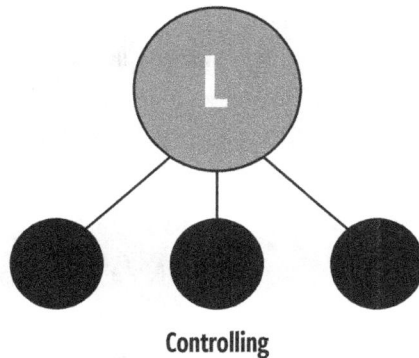

Controlling

I once worked as a sales director for a real estate services provider in Asia, where I experienced this level of engagement firsthand. When I commenced my role, the team-membership level was between three and four. The company was a start-up with big growth plans, and a group of us, all experienced in the industry, were brought in to run operations, marketing and sales. Initially we had tons of freedom to make decisions and the goal was clear: become the fastest-growing serviced-offices company in Asia. And we achieved that goal within two years. It was hard work, but rewarding.

Then things started to change. There seemed to be a natural mistrust by some senior people within a newly formed executive team, and suddenly decisions were taken away from us, even small ones. The CEO wanted to know everything, to the extent that salespeople had to blind-copy him in on all emails to clients. We were told that the company wanted open communication and to help employees improve. This was just an excuse to monitor every detail and micromanage everyone. We became more guarded with our opinions because we were publicly shamed if our views were different from those of a small group of people who had built a personal alliance with top management.

Staff turnover began to rise, and negativity and fear were palpable. People were hired on a whim, and if they didn't work out they were shown the door within their probation period. I started worrying, not sleeping well, and had anxiety attacks in the middle of the night, constantly fearing that I would be fired. Only when I left did I realise that this was a classic case of workplace bullying and certainly the most toxic culture I had ever experienced. The problem was systemic, and when I catch up with old colleagues now we still look back in disbelief at what happened to us in that organisation.

> 'THE CULTURE OF ANY ORGANISATION IS SHAPED BY THE WORST BEHAVIOUR THE LEADER IS WILLING TO TOLERATE.'
>
> —STEVE GRUENERT AND TODD WHITAKER

My experience within this organisation may be an extreme case, but this kind of behaviour and culture is more prevalent that many people realise. When destructive behaviour is allowed—or worse, actively encouraged—it creates a toxic workplace culture where people stop trusting each other, which in turn leads to invulnerability.

It all starts with trust

When there is a lack of trust, people put up armour to protect themselves. They avoid having conversations altogether, or they just share what they think the leaders want to hear. Team members stop bringing in ideas, decline to admit mistakes and avoid asking for help.

In his book, *The Five Dysfunctions of a Team*, Patrick Lencioni gives a clear illustration of those five dysfunctions, as shown in the following model.

Patrick Lencioni's five dysfunctions of a team

Lencioni explains that failure to build trust is damaging because it sets the tone for the second dysfunction: fear of conflict. Teams that lack trust resort to veiled discussions and guarded comments, exactly what I personally experienced in that job in Asia. He further explains that fear of conflict leads to a lack of commitment to goals or decisions. Without committing to a clear plan, team members hesitate to hold each other accountable, which can result in inattention to results. This occurs when team members put their individual needs, such as ego or recognition, ahead of everything else.

People fear a loss of control, and as a result can either leave an organisation or throw colleagues under the bus for their own gain. Destructive engagement and toxic cultures lead to underperformance and high staff turnover, which in turn impacts an organisation's performance. A research paper published at the National Institute of Health shows that there is a relation between workplace bullying and job performance.[12]

If you find yourself, your team or your organisation on this level in the team-member engagement model, the focus for getting to the next level is awareness. Humans are generally hardwired to find solutions and solve problems; consequently many leaders want to go directly from level 1 (destructive) to level 5 (agile). To make this transition successfully, however, it means changing focus and taking it step by step, in increments, along with the necessary change of focus. When all these things are put in place, the desired change will take place.

Creating self-awareness

If you think you're on this level, you've done part of the job already; you have observed and recognised the behaviour that is typical for this level. Self-awareness is about noticing what's going on in teams and organisations, where underperformance comes from, and what culture is present. But don't just focus on your team; take a look in the mirror first and create awareness about your own leadership style, your challenges and what you bring to the table.

I recommend that you get crystal clear on your strengths and challenges. Create a list of the strengths and focus on the top two or three while making your weaknesses irrelevant. Focusing on your strengths will help you to grow exponentially.

Check your level of wellbeing and resilience, and be more mindful when it comes to sleep, work-life balance and stress. We are often so focused on getting things done and hitting organisational goals that we forget we can't serve from an empty vessel.

Tuning in to your emotions and how you manage them is all part of emotional intelligence. (I explain how to develop those skills later in the book.) For your team members, you could use an employee-engagement survey, but because there is often a lack of trust on this level, the question is how honest people will be.

Be aware of your communication style. A great way to find out why you do what you do and how it impacts other people is to use a diagnostic tool like the popular DISC (dominance, influence, steadiness, compliance) assessment or Myers Briggs. Work with your coach or mentor to self-reflect, and put strategies in place to improve effectiveness of relationships and levels of communication.

On this level it's all about creating awareness of how your own state of mind, behaviour, conversations and decision-making impact team engagement, as well as helping your team members recognise the same for themselves.

Once you have created self-awareness, you're ready to move to level 2 of the team-member engagement model.

Level 2: Disengaged

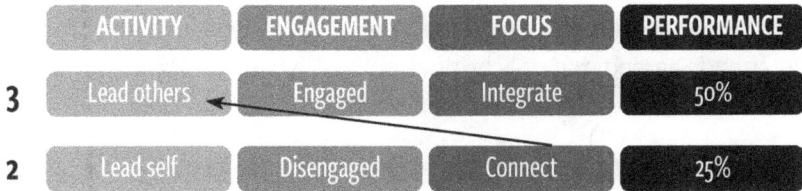

	ACTIVITY	ENGAGEMENT	FOCUS	PERFORMANCE
3	Lead others	Engaged	Integrate	50%
2	Lead self	Disengaged	Connect	25%

On level 2 of the value model, the activity is 'lead self'. On this level, individuals are generally happy with their own work, department or region, and their focus is largely on themselves. Interactions are pleasant and people are nice to each other, but relationships lack meaning and real connection. I describe team-member engagement on this level as 'disengaged'.

It's like grain silos in agriculture. Every silo is filled with unique products and remains apart from all the other silos. The silos can all be filled and emptied, but what happens in one silo doesn't affect the others. In organisations or teams, people can behave in the same way: their world of work doesn't intersect with the rest of the team or organisation. Employees and leaders make decisions without considering how they affect others. Just like grain silos, they stand in isolation and are less concerned with the overall goals of the team or organisation.

You can recognise this level when it feels like a number of individuals are working side by side in a group rather than in a team. It can be a tricky level to identify. On the surface the team can appear to be engaged, with individuals generally performing well and conversations friendly, but there can be too much focus on the individual team member and individual accountability. On this level, a team can be considered engaged but in reality it is disengaged.

In Hong Kong I coached an intact senior team in the IT industry, consisting of six regional directors who were in charge of sales and marketing for regions all across Asia and the Middle East. Their team leader, let's call him Peter, was head of sales and marketing. He brought me in to help create a more cohesive and engaged team, with the goal of increasing overall performance. The issue was that some directors were performing well in their regions while others fell short in reaching targets time and time again. Peter and I agreed that only by developing the team and team engagement would overall team performance be achieved.

I interviewed all individuals to gauge the level of team engagement, and my feeling early on was that the team was on level 2 of the model. Even during the individual interview rounds, when I spent sixty minutes with each leader, I felt like I was talking to six individual leaders that were almost entirely focused on themselves and their own success or challenges.

Over the next six months of team coaching and individual sessions, I was privileged to have in-depth insight into the team culture and behaviour that was holding the team back from hitting their targets as a collective.

To give you context about my work with this team, in coaching sessions I participated in live meetings to observe individual and team behaviour, and listened to conversations so I could intervene with reflection and feedback. The purpose was for everyone to create awareness of what they needed to change so they could become a more cohesive and effective team.

The team had two meetings for two hours each month using a digital platform, one focused on sales and the other focused on marketing. Here is what happened in the first sales meeting I attended.

Three of the six team members were late, one by as many as fifteen minutes, without offering an excuse. Peter started the meeting by going around the virtual room asking every team member for their regional update. Team members followed a structure, presenting on sales numbers and results for their region one by one, which took up almost the entire meeting. At the end there were no questions. There were some comments along the lines of 'Well done in your region', and a bit of banter in the chat thread and then the meeting came to an end.

Create meetings with purpose and people will engage

In my debriefing with Peter, I suggested a change to the structure of the next meeting, which would focus on marketing. I asked him to spend less time on updates and more time on discussing collective and individual challenges, and overall department goals. Peter changed the agenda accordingly and I was curious to see what would happen in the next meeting.

Despite Peter encouraging discussion and feedback, I noticed a lack of engagement by half the team. Their eyes wandered quite obviously, usually focusing on their second computer screen, and when put on the spot with questioning they struggled to come up with succinct answers. Some of the team members contributed to the discussion, but the discourse stayed superficial, with people agreeing with one another rather than challenging. I had the feeling that everyone would be content to finish the meeting so they could go on with their work.

The same behaviour showed up in other interactions, which is typical for level-2 team-member engagement. On this level, team members are nice to each other, but conversations lack depth. There is general nodding and agreement rather than people giving each other feedback and offering up their expertise and insights. Team members might give each other space to talk and present, but little time is spent on engaging in debate.

People on this level are focused on themselves and their own projects or work. They are generally good at achieving a healthy work-life balance and they manage their emotions well. Hitting targets and achieving their own goals are front and centre for them. Performance is only at twenty-five percent on this level.

Lencioni's model of the five dysfunctions of a team provides proof that 'inattention to results' equals 'underperformance of a team, and this comes from team members putting their own individual needs, like ego and recognition, above the collective goals of the team'.

The leadership style on this level can be described as 'coordinating'.

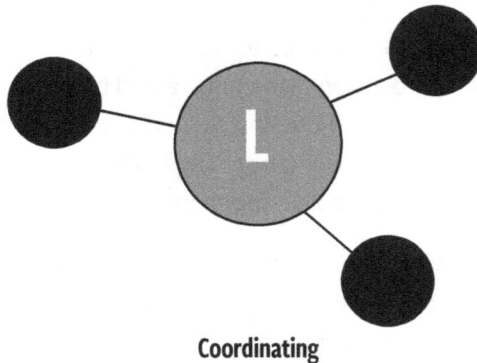

Coordinating

The leader distributes tasks to their reporting team and coordinates client work. Because of a lack of engagement, people don't share best practice and learn little from each other. Leaders are more senior because they are more experienced, but they play their cards close to their chests and find it hard to share knowledge. There is little focus on developing their reporting team members.

While some team members might hit targets, the team itself often underperforms on this level. The fear for the individual is of not belonging, and people leave because they don't feel valued or part of a meaningful purpose. Underperformance and staff attrition can be directly linked to this level of engagement.

According to a recent *Harvard Business Review* article, 'Engagement is a known driver of productivity.'[13] Interestingly, the authors of the article also found through a survey that while teams may sometimes appear to be engaged, it is on an individual level only. Individuals are keen to progress in their careers and they perform well. There is nothing wrong with this attitude as such, but when people are not invested in their teams it impacts team performance and culture.

If you find yourself on this level of engagement, either as a team leader or as someone in charge of developing an intact team in your organisation, the focus for you is 'connect' to be able to move from 'disengaged' to 'engaged'.

Connect means removing the silos everyone is working in. Start creating common goals the team can work towards. This is what Peter, my client from the IT firm, focused on first. He looked at his territory as a whole region rather than as six separate regions, and tasked his sales and marketing directors with formulating goals they needed to achieve together. I helped him with the structure and facilitated two team sessions where the team achieved this in collaborative fashion through a SWOT analysis (strength, weakness, opportunity, threat) and goal setting. My focus during these sessions was two-fold: to get the team to create goals, and to set parameters for their team performance, but to do it with the help of process. By process I mean learning how to use feedback, moving from conversation to debate, and engaging in constructive conflict.

The goals were in line with what the organisation had set out in terms of growth. With the company planning to list on the stock exchange, the stakes were high and the overall financial goals were clear. This gave the team a boost to work together and achieve more. The coaching sessions helped them adopt the right skills for the right conversations. It took this team a few months to change from being disengaged to being engaged, but they got there eventually by consistently working on communication and collaboration, and by working towards common goals.

It's not just about team members connecting and engaging with each other. It actually starts with the individual. Building trust is key to reaching level 3 of the model. According to an engagement survey by the ADP Research institute, 'Trust in team leaders is the foundation of Engagement. When we examined the most engaged teams, we found that by far the best explainer of level of Engagement was whether or not the team members trust their team leader. A worker is 12 times more likely to be fully Engaged if he or she trusts the team lead."[14]

Build trust through communication, feedback and social intelligence. (You will find practical tips on how to develop these key skills later in the book.) When you have created a culture of trust and have connected your people, you will be ready to move to level 3 of the team-member engagement model.

Level 3: Engaged

	ACTIVITY	ENGAGEMENT	FOCUS	PERFORMANCE
4	Lead change	Responsive	Co-create	75%
3	Lead others	Engaged	Integrate	50%

Level 3 of the team-member engagement model is similar to the way people behave on social media. On LinkedIn, for example, some people go through their feed regularly without interacting with the people who have posted. I call these people 'lurkers'. Others go a step further, liking some posts and commenting on others. These people look like they're engaged, but their impact is not great. I call these people 'players'.

However, when people create content through sharing their expertise and stories, ask their audience questions for feedback, and in turn comment on other peoples' posts consistently, that's when they are truly engaged. I call these people 'influencers'. Influencers not only benefit from giving and gaining expertise, but they also create trust and get other people involved in the conversation rather than just speaking *at* them. When it comes to engagement, the question is: are you a lurker, a player, or an influencer?

Engaging in teams and organisations is not so dissimilar to this LinkedIn example. When leaders and team members are engaged, they actively participate in team meetings and conversations, ask questions, and challenge the status quo. They do this not only for their own benefit, but also to achieve team and organisational goals.

You will know when your organisation is on this level when team members listen to each other, engage in debate, and don't avoid conflict. People give each other feedback, both positive and negative, in a productive way. Team members respect and value each other, and understand that team success comes from the team being more than the sum of its parts. There is a level of influence from the leader and also from team members, and everyone manages to stay connected and engaged in remote or hybrid set-ups.

In 2015 a regional vice president of an airline, let's call her Sarah, engaged me to work with her and her senior-leadership team in Asia. She had recently been promoted to take on this large region and an intact team of six team members, comprised of a mix of regional sales managers, PR and governance employees. She didn't engage me because there was a problem. The region was in fact performing well, but she knew that if she wanted to be successful and achieve the growth plans head office had set for the region for the coming year, she could only achieve this through her team stepping up; she knew it wasn't good enough to simply have an engaged team.

Appearing engaged is not being engaged

We started with assessments, individual interviews and a team survey. The results confirmed her initial thoughts. The team was on level 3 of the team-member engagement model. Although this value model didn't exist in its current form back then, the team's behaviours and interactions were proof of the team's strengths and challenges. The team was engaged, but members lacked the drive and strategies to realise the necessary change.

After some initial workshopping, we had our first team coaching session. I got the team to benchmark themselves in areas of communication, leadership style, approach to process, roles and productivity. They identified that they were about halfway on the path to being a high-performance team. They were then tasked to create some common goals to get from where they were to where they wanted to be, with organisational goals in mind.

This exercise wasn't just designed for benchmarking; it was also instructive in gauging how much self-awareness the team had, and what their individual strengths and opportunities were. I observed the interactions in the room during the session, and the behaviour was in line with team performance on level 3. Conversation flowed, team members were engaged, and team goals were agreed upon quite swiftly. Almost too swiftly. It was up to the team to decide what kind of goals to create, which they did, but I knew they were capable of more. If they had challenged each other more they would have seen more of a stretch. But team development doesn't happen in a day. It happens in stages.

Stop solving problems; empower your teams

In our subsequent session I sat in on the team's strategy meeting. The meeting was designed for Sarah to give high-level updates from head office, followed by the team's strategies for realising the company's goals in their region. The company had big growth plans, so there was ample opportunity for the team to step up.

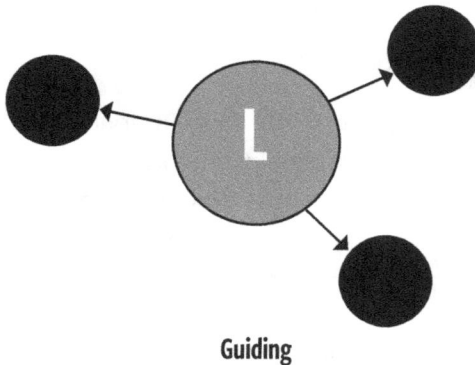

Guiding

This is what I saw. Although the team was engaged in conversation, Sarah led this conversation most of the time and had the most airtime, a scenario typical of this level of team-member engagement, where a 'guiding' leadership style is dominant. The leader takes a central role in the team, offering strong guidance on solutions and processes. Team members are involved and engaged, but not empowered to lead change.

After the meeting, I gave Sarah my feedback. 'You have too much airtime in your meetings,' I told her. 'You ask your team to drive change, but they don't actually have to think for themselves, and nor are they challenged by you or each other. Remember, this is their meeting, not yours.' Sarah told me that in the context of team-member engagement, this was a pivotal learning moment for her.

Sarah's one-on-one conversations with her team members about their day-to-day business were positive and practical. She gave balanced feedback, supported them when they needed it, and cascaded important information from head office regularly. But her team members kept running into problems they didn't seem to be able to solve by themselves, so she ended up stepping in time and time again to turn things around for them.

This type of process involves too much heavy lifting for a leader, and for team members it feels like back-delegating, which results in team members not feeling valued. In addition, they don't learn to think on their feet. The fears on this level involve lack of autonomy and capability. A lack of autonomy holds people back from realising their potential, and a lack of capability holds people back from making decisions with confidence.

Leading change versus managing change

When faced with change, or if they are under pressure, some people struggle on this level. They find complex decision-making difficult, and team members often lack the confidence to step up quickly and adapt to change. In our current world of constant and fast change, these capabilities are crucial; your job as a leader is develop these skills.

Other team members might thrive on this level while still feeling that they're not empowered to drive change. These people either leave to find a job where they are challenged, or stay but are held back through not realising their potential.

In the context of the team-member engagement model, this level is halfway to becoming a leader or team that leads the future. The trick here is to not get confused by the impact an engaged team member or team has. As I've mentioned, it has been proven that high team-member engagement impacts positively on performance, but in the model performance is only at the level of fifty percent out of one hundred percent. In other words, they are only halfway there.

You might even refer to the results of your recent employee engagement and think people are happy and engaged, and the feedback supports that, but engagement from the point of view of your team members is only one side of the story. As a leader, you know what the next ten years will look like and what level of engagement is needed to be successful. You might have achieved the level of engaged, but there are two more steps necessary before you're able to lead the future.

This level is not a bad position to be in, but for an organisation undergoing substantial change, being exposed to the VUCA world (e.g. Covid-19 crisis) or having big growth plans, this level of engagement doesn't suffice.

The focus to get to the next level of team-member engagement is 'integrate'. As a team leader, this means becoming part of the team rather than heading up the team.

Sarah followed my advice and changed the way she conducted strategy meetings. She designed the agenda in such a way that head office updates were made available before meetings so everyone could familiarise themselves with them. She then set her expectations for the team, which involved coming up with suggestions and solutions for each of the strategies during the meeting. She still facilitated the conversation, but ensured that airtime was distributed equally, with everyone contributing. As a result of these changes, her team members felt empowered and challenged, and the team worked collectively towards a common goal.

Avoid back-delegating

Integrating means using your team's potential, getting everyone on the same page, and creating strong common goals. You also have to think about other teams in the organisation, how they are impacted and how they can help you. As one team, you are still only a small cog in a larger system, and without integrating yourself or your team you run the danger of being too isolated from the rest of the organisation.

I recently ran a team coaching session with a government department in the UK, in which people came up with practical strategies to integrate into the wider team. They decided to bring other leaders into their strategy meetings and create roundtable discussions with other senior stakeholders.

For your one-on-one relationships, learn how to delegate. Take the time and a coaching approach so your team members can learn how to solve problems, take the initiative, and think on their feet. You'll find that they have the potential, and often the solution; you just need to tease it out of them.

I worked with a large retailer in Australia a few years ago where we taught store managers to ask their staff several open questions when presented with a problem. This coaching approach doubled team-member engagement in stores and saved managers valuable time, which they could use to lead rather than put out fires. A few suggestions for open questions:

- What is the problem?
- What would you like instead?
- What is one thing you could do?
- What have you done in the past that worked?
- What have you seen other people do that solved the problem?
- What is your first step? When will you take it?

If you want your team members and teams to step up the next level, work autonomously, lead change and make the right business decisions, empower them to do so, and develop them as individuals so they have the skills. Once you've focused on integrating your team you'll be ready to move onto level 4 of the team-member engagement model.

Level 4: Responsive

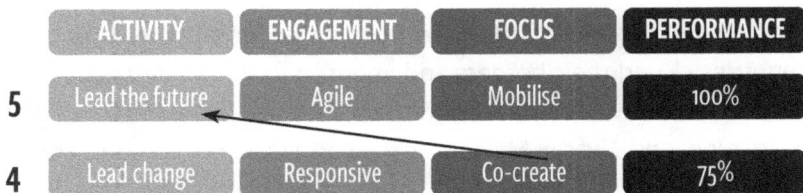

	ACTIVITY	ENGAGEMENT	FOCUS	PERFORMANCE
5	Lead the future	Agile	Mobilise	100%
4	Lead change	Responsive	Co-create	75%

On level 4 of the value model, the team-member engagement level is 'responsive'. This reminds me of going to the local summer fair with my sister and grandmother when I was six years old. My favourite game at the fair was where we sat in front of a large disc with seven holes the size of teacup saucers, and in quick succession a clown's head would pop up out of one of the holes. We each had a hammer, and the aim was to whack the head with the hammer to gain a point. (This game is known as Whac-A-Mole in gaming arcades). We had to react fast to keep up, and my sister and I got quite competitive with the number of clowns we were able to whack.

In the VUCA business world of today, we are faced with many challenges that are popping up like clowns' heads out of nowhere. I described some of these drivers of change in the megatrends earlier in the book. The ability to react and respond to these changes has become key for leaders if they want to be successful. In a race to stay relevant, we must adapt to consumer trends, technological advancements, and the changing DNA of our workforce.

During my time in Asia, after I left the real estate firm I worked for a company that designed and delivered experiential study tours for postgraduate business-school students. The students typically travelled to an overseas destination to learn firsthand how business was done successfully internationally. The student groups visited businesses and factories, attended lectures and presentations, and took part in cultural immersions. The organisation's head office was located in Prague, with a team of seventy sales and operations staff who organised over two hundred study trips a year. I headed up business development in the Hong Kong office and worked closely with universities all across Asia. I was still consulting for them part time when the Covid-19 pandemic hit in 2020.

Adapt quickly to serve clients and stay relevant

I remember the initial shock and ongoing uncertainty as, one by one, countries closed their borders and imposed lockdown restrictions. One particular moment stands out, which I mentioned in the introduction but bears repeating. I was in Melbourne guiding a group of students from the United States. They were called back to the US only two days into the program out of fear that the Centers for Disease Control and Prevention would shut the US borders to incoming travellers. It was obvious that things were getting serious, and a few days later the World Health Organization declared Covid-19 a global pandemic.

All immediate and future trips the company had confirmed were cancelled, and within a few days it was clear the situation wasn't going to change anytime soon. The challenges were two-fold. We had to ensure that students who were enrolled in programs for that year could still graduate, and the organisation's leaders were tasked with figuring out how the business could survive. Task forces and project groups were created, and over the following weeks plans were put in place.

We adapted by using our global network of lecturers and speakers to create online learning experiences for students. We implemented and tested the technology and vetted our speakers. We trained staff to moderate the sessions and organise the logistics so students had the most authentic learning experience, and the sessions ran without a hitch. We helped hundreds of students to finish the semester and gain credit for their coursework.

Knowing that international travel would be out of question for some time, other opportunities and ideas were formulated in brainstorming sessions and design-thinking workshops. It was clear that we had to take advantage of the digital world. There was a huge appetite for experiential learning, not only in universities but also in businesses all over the world, and we could bring this to people on digital-learning platforms. Virtual study tours and online group consulting projects were designed for students, and a whole new company was formed that focused on creating and delivering hackathons.

We were able to achieve this through leaders keeping team members engaged. This meant sustained engagement and encouragement to get involved in new projects. Teams responded to the changes quickly, adapted to new situations and ways of doing things (everyone in the company became a salesperson), and people learned how to solve complex problems by collaborating and innovating.

That's what you typically see on this level of team-member engagement. You know you're on this level when you and your team respond well to change, can navigate your workforce in a VUCA world, and have the skills to use technological advances to change your business model when needed.

The leadership style on this level is typically 'empowering'.

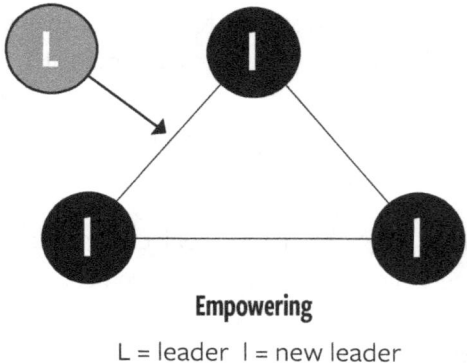

Empowering

L = leader I = new leader

On this level, the leader oversees the day-to-day business, but has a strong, autonomous team. As the graphic illustrates, the job of a leader in this style is to develop and empower new leaders who go on to lead their own projects, departments or teams. It's a collaborative effort between leaders and team leaders.

On the empowering level of team-member engagement, there is great belief in the potential of team members, plus a focus on enabling people to use their strengths to influence their own teams, take initiative, make autonomous decisions, and lead change.

Leaders and team members on this level have highly effective internal meetings, are goal driven, and adapt well to changes in the environment. There is also a high level of delegation and accountability, which increases the team's productivity and enables the team leader to work *on* the business rather than *in* the business, and to work more strategically. Team members are able to work autonomously and have the skill and confidence to solve problems independently.

This is not a bad level of team-member engagement to be on. Performance is at seventy-five percent and chances are the organisation will be able to adapt to future changes. But there is one more step. If you find yourself on level 4 (responsive), your focus to lead the future is 'co-create.'

Lead the future by co-creating

'Integrate' was about getting people on the same page and developing strategies and capabilities to react and adapt to change. 'Co-create' is more dynamic and future orientated. If you want to lead the future, you can't wait for change to happen. You need foresight to shape the future. (I explain the skill of foresight later in the book.) Put simply, the key to foresight is watching trends rather than events and envisioning and developing scenarios for the future.[15]

This kind of future thinking and acting doesn't happen in a vacuum. To lead the future successfully, you need co-create it with your employees, clients, stakeholders, and government and industry bodies. Let's look at the example of co-creating future hybrid workspaces.

At the time of writing, employees all around the world have been forced to work from home for at least some part of the last eighteen months. With vaccinations underway and restrictions easing, knowledge workers are now returning to a situation that has been described as the 'next normal'. Organisations across the world are downsizing and reconfiguring their office space. This means substantial cost savings for companies and a reduction in their carbon footprint, and it also offers unique opportunities to design workspaces that support a particular work culture and enable productivity. I suggest you co-create your workspaces with your employees.

Doing hybrid right with the human in mind

How are we enticing people to come back to the office? I recently discussed this issue with a global leader of a Melbourne-based engineering company. Workers within his company had been slow to return to the office, with attendance below fifty percent. The company decided to downsize the office floorplate by half and signed a lease in a new building. The engineering leader was part of the project team that designed the space, and he asked me what they should consider for their hybrid office design.

The first thing I said was that simply having a smaller office space but shipping over the old furniture and having an app for employees to register desk space did not represent flexible, hybrid working. I encouraged him to discuss the kind of work culture they wanted, not just with the executive team but also with the entire workforce in the region.

The engineering leader and I then talked about purpose. I knew his company employed a large number of young engineers. Younger generations have a real need for connecting to a purpose, so I challenged him to be clear on what that purpose was for them, and to design a space that was centred on a culture and purpose.

In his case, I suggested he consider creating an innovation hub right in the middle of the space, where people had access to some of their new AI technology, and where they could collaborate and innovate the engineering of the future.

There were so many interesting innovations going on in this organisation. 'I think you need to make this accessible,' I suggested, 'and have senior people like yourself in the space regularly to share your knowledge and opportunities in a collaborative environment.' This would get people excited and make them come to the workspace, where they could experience innovation and creation firsthand.

In your own organisation, ask your team members what they want to come back to. Consider not even calling it an office if people don't want to come back to an office. Call it a work hub, a co-working space, an innovation hub, a satellite space … anything that's in line with the reasons why people would want to be there.

If innovating your products is part of your vision and future plan, co-create a workplace where innovating and visioning are front and centre of the space, interactions and your culture. Co-create with your employees as well as clients and industry bodies to shape the future of work, not just for yourselves but also for your community or even the world.

When you co-create well, you will move up to the next and highest level of the team-member engagement model, which is 'agile'.

Level 5: Agile

	ACTIVITY	ENGAGEMENT	FOCUS	PERFORMANCE
5	Lead the Future	Agile	Mobilise	100 %

On this highest level of team-member engagement, you and your team proactively make decisions and action those with a long-term view to future-proofing your business for your employees and the community, if not the whole world.

Here in Australia, many couples plan their children's future from the day they are born, often enrolling their children in school when they are still very young. The school system is very competitive, and those who want their children to attend their public school of choice need to live in a certain catchment area. Private schools are expensive and often difficult to get into, so early planning is necessary.

What these parents do is envisage their children's future; specifically, the opportunities they want their children to have. They consider future trends like what the jobs of the future will look like and therefore what skills will be necessary. For instance, many parents are eager for their children to learn different languages like Spanish, Japanese or Mandarin to be competitive in a more globalised world.

I have seen parents go through extensive research into specialised skills programs in sports or STEM (science, technology, engineering, math) to enable their children to be successful in a fast-changing work environment. People will often mobilise their whole family, change their own jobs and leave their communities to move into a particular catchment area so they enrol their children in the perfect school to set them up for success. The future of their children, which will impact their own lives one day, is extremely important to these parents, so they move heaven and earth to future-proof their children's lives.

Leading the future is not so dissimilar. Leaders on this level envisage the future. They envisage the future not just for themselves or their own organisation, but also with regard to what the industry, community or world will look like. Leaders on this level are hyper-aware of the 5 Megatrends, how they impact the present, and will shape the future.

Agile is the superpower for the future

A good example of a long-term view and vision of the future is the story of the people behind the popular outdoors sports-clothing brand, Patagonia. The founders started out making pitons for rock climbing so people could explore wild places, which led the company to the conclusion that they should also be in the business of protecting wild places.

Patagonia now sells everything from outdoor clothing to surfing wetsuits, sleeping bags and backpacks. Their mission statement: *Patagonia is in business to save our home planet.* The people behind the brand know that if we don't change the way we live now, the consequences for humans will be dire in the future. They envision a future that is not just about sustainable clothing, but also clothing that doesn't cause chemical harm to the environment, and leaves rivers and oceans unpolluted and clean. The company also mobilised their production and supply chain to use only organic cotton.

Patagonia donates one percent of their sales to grassroots environmental organisations (approximately $20 million annually) and spends more time advocating for environmental causes than marketing their own products. And as a result their business continues to thrive.[16]

To be on this level of engagement, team members and leaders have to be agile. In Patagonia's example, the leaders knew that the right thing to do was switch to organic cotton to stay true to their mission and vision, but at first they had no idea how to get there.

Agility starts with an agile mindset, for which Susan McIntosh created a comprehensive definition. An agile mindset is a set of attitudes supporting an agile working environment. These include respect, collaboration, improvement and learning cycles, pride in ownership, focus on delivering value, and the ability to adapt to change. This mindset is necessary to cultivate high-performing teams, which in turn deliver amazing value for their customers.[17]

The leadership style you often find on this level of team-member engagement is 'inspiring'.

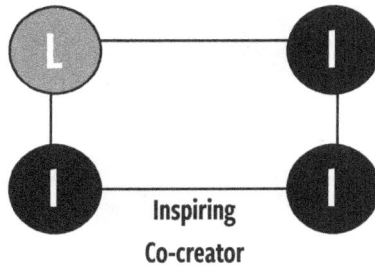

Inspiring
Co-creator

L = leader   I = new leaders

A leader is part of the team and inspires their people to be leaders in their own right. In other words, leaders are creators of new leaders. This can only happen through trust and empowerment, which is often found on this level of team-member engagement. Leaders are able to inspire their teams, and co-create solutions and future visions in open, psychologically safe environments. They encourage participation, and they also want their people to use their initiative.

If you want to mobilise your team or organisation, or even a whole industry (imagine every clothing label being more like Patagonia) influencing needs to shift to mobilising. It's like influencing on steroids, where everyone believes in the mission and visions, from the receptionist to the executive, the retail customer to the wholesale buyer, the investor to the government official.

CHAPTER 3

THE FOUR STAGES OF LEADING THE FUTURE

W e seem to be moving into a new world at the speed of light. Globalisation, technological progress and the current global health crisis have put a huge amount of pressure on leaders; however, these challenges also present opportunities to create more flexibility in the workplace and renewed purpose in organisations. Technological disruption is shaping the future of work. Many people think that machines will take their jobs, but it's all about human skills because these are what shape the way we embrace disruption and create the workplace of the 21st century.

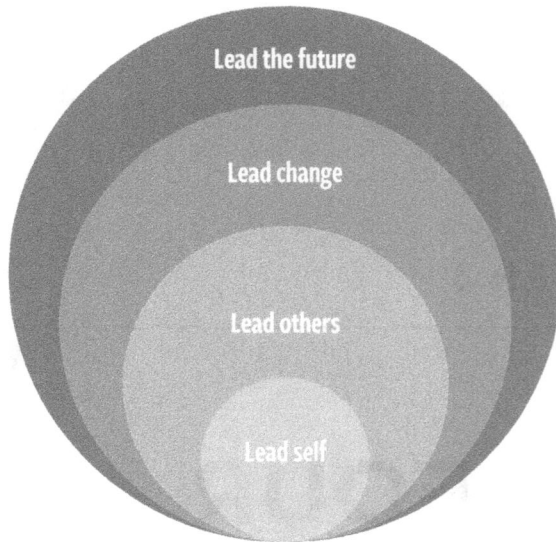

The 4 pillars of leadership

The pandemic has caused a significant shift in the way people work. As work arrangements are restructured, companies are finding that they need to navigate distributed teams and remote employees who have embraced flexibility in their work and personal lives. The new model of hybrid working comes with challenges. There has been a drop in team-member engagement and a change in productivity. There is too much emphasis on structure and process, and not enough focus on leading people.

What's needed is renewed focus on equipping people with the right leadership skills to help them increase engagement, lead change and lead the future. I have developed a model comprising the 12 Skills necessary to lead in a fast-changing and ambiguous world. These skills are based on the 4 Pillars of Leadership: lead self, lead others, lead change, and lead the future.

THE 4 PILLARS OF LEADERSHIP

Pillar 1: Lead Self

There is a general misconception that leadership is always something that is done to other people. In fact, successful and impactful leadership of others always includes and starts with leading self. Research in *Psychology Today* shows that thirty percent of Fortune 500 leaders last less than three years. Why? Because they are not good at leading self. I believe that regardless of our title or position, strong self-leadership is the foundation of success, happiness and resilience, in both our personal and professional lives.[18]

> 'AS A LEADER, THE FIRST PERSON I NEED TO LEAD IS ME. THE FIRST PERSON THAT I SHOULD TRY TO CHANGE IS ME.'
>
> —JOHN C MAXWELL

Leading self reminds me of a bucket that has holes. If you keep filling up the bucket with water without fixing the holes, the bucket will never stay full. You have to fix the holes first, and then you can fill up your bucket. You can only serve from a full bucket.

Leading self is all about mindset. I once coached a regional director in the retail industry, let's call him Thomas, who had been with the company for over a decade. He had started as an assistant manager in one of the stores and worked his way up. His operational expertise was second to none, but the feedback from his direct reports showed a big gap in his leadership.

People feared asking Thomas questions because he could be dismissive, and they felt he didn't support them when they had challenges with other departments. He was often late, or postponed important one-on-one meetings at the last minute. People didn't feel a connection because he was always in a rush and his dealings with other people were very transactional. He was nice, but he didn't give employees enough constructive feedback to enable them to excel at their jobs.

Thomas was surprised about the feedback. He prided himself on the industry experience he had, and for always achieving results for his region. He said that he led the way he had learned from his former leaders: get things done, don't accept laziness, and work hard. This is an archaic model of control-and-command leadership that lost its effectiveness a long time ago.

I helped Thomas look at the feedback objectively. People were simply telling him how they saw him according to their reality. They liked him, but they needed him to change before they could work more effectively. To become an effective team member, he had to change his mindset, get some perspective on what his strengths were, and find out what was holding him back. His results were hitting the mark, but he turned over sixty percent of his managers.

Thomas and I unpacked the feedback over a number of coaching sessions, and he realised it was up to him to change his approach. He worked on his emotional intelligence and replaced verbal outbursts with listening and understanding. He focused on delegating and empowering his direct reports instead of back-delegating. This was all hard for him because in his mind it felt like a loss of control, but he realised that his managers were intelligent and capable people who were thriving on being truly accountable.

Thomas asked his assistant to help him with scheduling, making one-on-one conversations a priority, and he adopted some techniques for giving regular feedback. He also made time for his people to get to know who he was, as a private person. He was surprised at how easy it was to share personal details, and how it increased trust between himself and the people around him.

It wasn't easy for Thomas to change. He had to change his old belief system and mindset regarding what leadership was, and to realise that it all started with himself.

Leading yourself involves understanding your feelings, beliefs and values and how they influence the decisions you make and how you interact with others. Without having an awareness of yourself, and your natural high preferences when it comes to behaviour and communication, it's impossible to improve relationships with others. Create self-awareness of your inner narrative, your mindset and your core strengths, and ask for feedback from others to get an accurate view of the way people think of you.

This pillar focuses on leading with emotional intelligence, courage, resilience, and strength-based leadership. (I cover these skills in more depth later in the book.)

Pillar 2: Lead Others

The second pillar focuses on connection. When you lead other people, it's not just about you anymore. You need to tune into others and connect with them, and also connect team members with each other.

> 'YOU DON'T LEAD BY POINTING AND TELLING PEOPLE SOME PLACE TO GO. YOU LEAD BY GOING TO THAT PLACE AND MAKING A CASE.'
>
> —KEN KESEY

Leading others is like being a conductor of an orchestra. To create a perfect symphony, the conductor needs to know all the different players, and the sound of their instruments and how they should be played. The conductor also needs to direct the individuals, smaller groups and the orchestra as a whole. If the musicians don't connect with each other and the music, the result will be a group of musicians simply playing their own individual tunes.

> 'THE WHOLE IS MORE THAN THE SUM OF ITS PARTS.'
>
> —ARISTOTLE

I once worked with a business owner, let's call him Lloyd, of a small creative agency with fifteen employees. Lloyd had engaged me to help him manage the growth of the company. Their client portfolio was doubling, and he was in the process of hiring ten new designers and account managers. His employees were competent and great with clients, which let him focus on what he loved doing the most—implementing systems and software applications to automate processes for a smooth-running business. With the expansion, he needed everyone to step up, including himself, and he wasn't sure how to tackle that.

The problem was that although his team members worked well as individuals, they didn't work well as a team. There was a communication gap between account managers and creatives, resulting in project delays and clients not receiving the quality of work they had been promised. People were nice to each other, but they didn't collaborate. The lockdowns in Australia during 2020 meant team members were working in silos, which only made things worse.

Once everyone had returned to the office, I worked with Lloyd to formulate a strategy to connect everyone in the business. He hired an operations manager to take over systems and day-to-day operating processes, which freed him to work *on* the business, instead of getting involved too much *in* the business. He promoted his strongest managers to lead two teams—client management and creative management—and invested in coaching and training. The operations manager and the two leaders learned how to work together as an executive team and work towards common goals. They met regularly but led their teams independently.

Leading with a coaching approach, delegating, and creating a feedback culture were only some of the new capabilities we applied to lead strong teams. We also ran workshops with all team members to increase trust, connection and collaboration through skills training and team building.

For me, these are fundamentals of leadership. What has changed is the mode of working, and leaders have to learn to lead others, and connect in remote and hybrid work models. When people are physically apart, they can easily become disconnected. Team members have become quite efficient in using online platforms to communicate, but running team meetings effectively online is often a challenge. Senior executives have been asking me to help with group workshopping and solving complex problems when working virtually as they find these tasks less effective when using digital platforms.

This pillar focuses on leading in a hybrid world, feedback and productive conflict, and communication and influencing. (I share strategies and tools for these skills later in the book.)

Pillar 3: Lead Change

The third pillar is all about relevance. Leading change means making decisions that impact teams and organisations, and connecting the two with external factors like the 5 Megatrends covered earlier. The people who lead change anticipate change, and make relevant decisions considering clients, products and services, and project and communication strategies. Like an excursion leader of a group exploring unknown territory, these people lead from the front, scouting out safe routes

---

and looking for danger. They make sure to find the safest and fastest path to the destination, dealing with changes and freeing up the track for the group along the way.

> ' OUR ONLY SECURITY IS THE ABILITY TO CHANGE.'
>
> —JOHN LILLY

A good friend of mine, Jeremy, is national operations director of a popular food chain in Australia. He used to be my boss when I worked in hospitality in Sydney years ago. He is one of the best managers I have ever had, and leads himself and others well. He has a high level of emotional intelligence, stays calm under pressure, motivates and supports his teams, and runs operations like clockwork.

During the pandemic, Australia, and especially my home city of Melbourne, have been exposed to some of the strictest and longest lockdowns in the world, which has had a wide impact on the retail food industry. Some Australian cities have had multiple lockdowns, and Jeremy and his team have been agile enough to lead the change fast and effectively every single time.

Jeremy's organisation had to shut down most of their restaurants with only a few days' notice, restructure their workforce, supply chains and marketing, and shift food sales to home delivery. This is a great example of a company solving complex problems, reacting to changing circumstances quickly, and making relevant decisions to stay and thrive in business, swiftly implementing change-management strategies to keep their employees and customers safe.

This pillar focuses on leaders being adaptable, agile, and exceptional at complex problem-solving and change management. (I cover these skills in greater depth later in the book.)

Pillar 4: Lead the Future

The fourth pillar represents innovation. This is where leaders envision the future, foresee trends and changes in the world, innovate by embracing technology, and mobilise large numbers of people.

> ' THE GREATEST DANGER FOR MOST OF US IS NOT THAT OUR AIM IS TOO HIGH, AND WE MISS IT, BUT THAT IT IS TOO LOW, AND WE REACH IT.'
>
> —MICHELANGELO

I often think about the time Bill Gates and Steve Wozniak changed the world. A computer on every desk in every home was Microsoft's early mission. It was a bold, ambitious and life-changing goal. Microsoft envisioned an environment that didn't exist then and resembled somewhat of an impressionistic painting that was tangible enough to help them realise their vision. They didn't translate that vision into a winning strategy by building computers; they achieved it by scaling Satya Nadella's belief that leaders don't just lead people and teams; they develop people to become leaders themselves. This led to Miscrosoft employees being willing to trust, and the company went on to change the world for each and every one of us forever. Microsoft did indeed build computers for every desk in every home.

This is one of the most famous stories of envisioning, innovating and mobilising the world, and is a wonderful example of two people showing how to lead the future.

The last two pillars—Lead Change and Lead the Future—represent a real step up for leaders. The skills necessary in the first two pillars—Lead Self and Lead Others—are fundamental leadership skills, although the focus is on leading distributed teams; however, the skills necessary for the last two pillars are relatively new tools in many leaders' toolboxes. This is not to say that leaders have lacked adaptability and agility before now, but with the pace at which the world is changing, leaders need to focus like a laser beam on skills that matter to lead this VUCA world.

> 'I START WITH THE PREMISE THAT THE FUNCTION OF LEADERSHIP IS TO PRODUCE MORE LEADERS, NOT MORE FOLLOWERS.'
>
> —RALPH NADER

You won't be able to lead change and the future effectively without mastering the fundamentals. You won't be able to mobilise your workforce without having the ability to influence people. You won't be able to solve complex problems with your teams if you haven't mastered this ability in a remote work environment. And you won't be able to sell a vision if you don't know what you bring to the table.

Start with Pillar 1: Lead Self.

CHAPTER 4

THE 12 SKILLS NEEDED TO LEAD THE FUTURE

W ithin the four pillars of leadership are 12 skills crucial to leading the future. They are not the only ones to be displayed or developed through leadership roles, but they do form the backbone of a resilient and agile leader. Some are foundational to any level of leadership, like emotional intelligence, communicating and influencing, and giving and receiving feedback. They are probably not new to you. However some of the skills under the pillars 'lead change' and 'lead the future' might be less familiar to you.

Leading people in a hybrid world requires an increased level of emotional intelligence, not just the ability to implement the most suitable digital platform. Diving deep into these essential skills, set out here with practical frameworks and steps, will assist you to master and fine-tune these skills, then lead change effectively in the future.

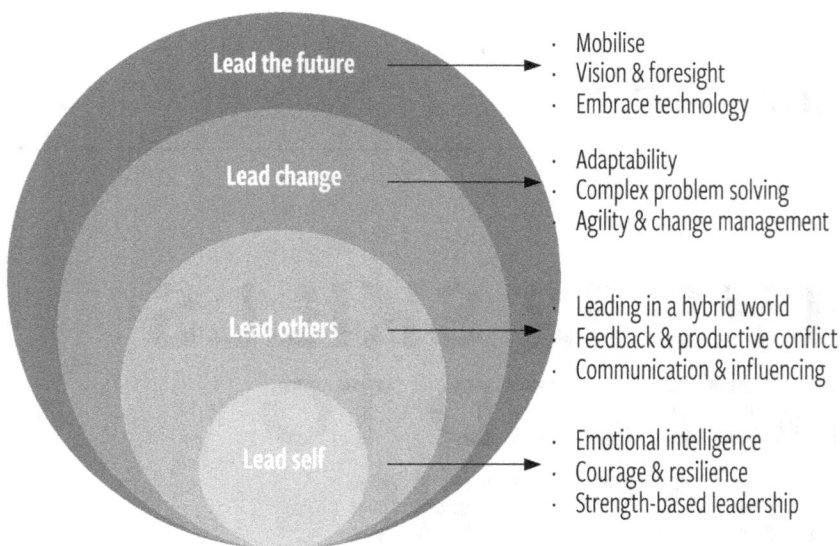

Lead the future
- Mobilise
- Vision & foresight
- Embrace technology

Lead change
- Adaptability
- Complex problem solving
- Agility & change management

Lead others
- Leading in a hybrid world
- Feedback & productive conflict
- Communication & influencing

Lead self
- Emotional intelligence
- Courage & resilience
- Strength-based leadership

The 12 skills to lead in a fast changing and ambiguous world, based on the 4 pillars of leadership

SKILL 1: STRENGTH-BASED LEADERSHIP

If we want to grow as leaders, we need to know where our greatest potential lies to be the best leader we can. Leading self starts with knowing our strengths and using these as our superpowers. This is more important than ever before as we find ourselves being challenged by a fast-changing and volatile environment; we have to build strong leadership foundations so that we, and our teams, can navigate the complexity and dynamism of today's business world.

A regional leader of a large bank once said to participants in one of my online workshops: 'If you want to grow as a leader and advance in your career, you have to know what you bring to the table.'

Why is it that we almost always focus on our weaknesses and often ignore our strengths? Why is it that we're so aware of our weaknesses but are not clear about our strengths? One reason could be that we have been brought up that way. During our formal early education, teachers and parents maybe have focused on our least favourable grades. And later on in our professional lives, in our performance reviews our managers possibly drilled down on our challenges as areas in need of growth.

When it comes to education and work performance, focusing on weaknesses is often ingrained in our habits. We might put a lot of effort into growing intellectually and professionally, yet still manage to focus on the one thing that holds us back from reaching our full potential: our weaknesses. It doesn't make sense.

The competitive sports world figured this out a long time ago. If a professional swimmer's strongest discipline is freestyle and their weakest is breaststroke, the swim coach is not going to focus on improving breaststroke marginally, leaving the swimmer still unable to win the heat. They will focus on freestyle in order to *win*.

Use your strengths for exponential growth

I love the work that Marcus Buckingham, a globally recognised speaker and business consultant, does around strength-based leadership.[19] He says that focusing on our weaknesses only enables us to achieve incremental improvement. Focusing on our strengths and playing to our strengths will bring us exponential growth. In his book, *Now Discover Your Strengths*, he busts some myths about strengths. Some of my examples are based on his research.

Surveys show that seventy-five percent of professionals believe they will be most successful if they focus on their weaknesses. But how can a focus on something perceived as a weakness help us succeed? When we're bad at something and we work really hard to get better at it, the outcome will be that we are just *less* bad at it than before. We will never be great at it.

Focusing on weaknesses, trying to invert them and expecting success ... it just doesn't work like that. Focusing on weaknesses enables incremental growth only. The greatest opportunity for growth comes from strengths.

There is a general misconception that strengths are only those things that we are good at and weaknesses are only those things that we are bad at. Buckingham busts that myth: 'Strengths are activities that make us feel strong, and weaknesses are activities that make us feel weak.' This concept is helpful for strengths-finding exercises; instead of picking talents from a list, we need to think about what makes us feel strong.

We can be good at something, but if it doesn't light us up and we hate doing it, it is in fact a weakness. That's when people say: *I'm really good at my job, but I hate it*. That's not sustainable. You can be bad at something but really love it. We would call that a hobby.

I wanted to be a journalist in my early twenties so I started an arts degree and took on a freelance job at the local newspaper. I loved going to the interviews, and I was good at getting people to trust me and share their stories, but writing the articles was really hard for me and I took longer than any other journalist at the office. I loved that job, but it was clear that writing was not my strength so I changed my career.

You might ask, how then did I write this book? Well, I actually discovered that I am a speaker who writes, so I recorded large parts of the book and then edited the transcripts. I used my strength as a great narrator to achieve the same outcome: publishing a book.

Knowing what your strengths are

People can often find it difficult to identify their strengths because they perceive them as negative. Strengths are neither good nor bad. They are value neutral. For example, if someone is a direct communicator they might come across as brash and abrupt and only be seen from that perspective, but this can also be a strength and help them achieve fast and precise outcomes.

It's about knowing when to play to a particular strength. It's a matter of perception: every strength, if overplayed, can be considered a weakness. What applies to you also applies to your team. Help your team members get clear on their strengths and build on where their shoulders are the broadest.

I worked with a leader who had taken over a new team of five account managers in the media industry. Two were really good at solving technical problems for clients and loved getting involved when things went wrong. The other three excelled at big-picture thinking and finding creative solutions. The team decided to distribute the work and responsibilities based on their strengths rather than general job descriptions. When I checked in after twelve months, the team not only had been hitting targets, but they had also grown the department by forty percent. Focusing on strengths for exponential growth also works for teams, not just individuals.

Make your weaknesses irrelevant

People often ask how they can fix their weaknesses. Buckingham's answer is: 'You don't fix them; you make them irrelevant.' Admittedly, we all have parts of our jobs or businesses that make us feel weak. For me, these are administration tasks, bookkeeping and systems. It's not a huge part, but I hate it. Instead of focusing my energy on those tasks in a negative way, I simply acknowledge them, get them out of the way first thing in the morning or while I'm watching TV (it's all shallow work for me) and outsource the rest to my business manager and bookkeeper. I can't eliminate that work, so I just make it irrelevant.

The beautiful thing about being clear about your strengths is knowing they are transferrable. You take them with you into your next role. In fact, they will *get* you your next role. When I coach people to help them achieve a career goal, I always challenge them to identify the strength they think will help them succeed. For example, I coached an executive in the banking industry who was striving for a strategic role, and advised him to focus on the strengths that helped him to be a strategic leader. This gave him clarity and a narrative with which to sell himself in the interviews.

I have developed the five following practical steps to leverage strengths for exponential growth:

Step 1   *Awareness: Find out what your strengths and weaknesses are. You might think that others are the best judges of your strengths. After all, your teachers, parents and managers have probably told you what your strengths are. But while it's always good to get an outside perspective, the work on awareness has to come from you.*

   Here is what I suggest. Based on the fact that a strength activity is something that makes you feel strong, consider your activities (at work) and look at how you feel before, during and after doing the activity. Divide your responses into categories: I feel strong when ... I feel weakened when ... Use a strengths list to help you with strength words. Ask people around you, from work and in your personal life, to give you feedback on why they like working with you. Use online assessment tools to help you, such as VIA Institute on Character.[20]

You can do a combination of strengths finding, but make sure the strengths line up with activities that make you feel strong.

Step 2   *Choice: Make an intentional choice about what you want to focus on, either your strengths or your weaknesses. Remember, you have a choice. If you're made to do activities all day that make you feel weak, you might want to consider whether doing these activities, or the job, is right for you.*

Step 3   *Focus: Less is more. Get crystal clear on the strengths and activities you want to make front and centre in your life. It might be difficult to implement and work on all your strengths, so I suggest you start by determining your two top strengths and make them your superpowers.*

My peer coaches gave me my coaching superpowers when I completed my coaching accreditation: they were confidence and warmth. I was surprised by warmth, not because I don't think I am warm, but because I didn't think it would be one of my two top strengths. But that's one of the reasons why people engage me as a coach. I am confident holding people in coaching conversations, and my warmth creates trust and helps them to be vulnerable and open up.

Step 4   *Plan: Develop a strategy to leverage your strengths; continue to do these activities and more often. Try to do them more intentionally, and make sure others in your team and organisation know you have these strengths. You also want to encourage your leaders to leverage off your strengths. Develop your strengths by learning a new skill around that strength. You could take a course or read literature. When you focus on your strengths with intent and build on them, you are more likely to focus your career or business around them. Get it out of your head and onto paper.*

Step 5   *Implement: Do one activity intentionally that frees up a particular strength, or stop one activity that holds that strength back. If you're like me, you might find it difficult to do this on your own. Find an accountability partner—coach, mentor or leader—and make them hold you accountable for not just talking about your strengths but using them intentionally as well. Start perceiving your weakness from a different perspective. Sometimes we have to do something we don't like, but if we see the greater good we just get on with it. We make our weaknesses irrelevant to our success.*

'YOUR STRENGTHS ARE WHAT GIVE YOU TRACTION BECAUSE THEY ALLOW YOU TO DO THE THINGS YOU DO WELL ALREADY. FOCUSING ON ANYTHING ELSE JUST LEADS TO SPINNING YOUR WHEELS.'

—SEAN CHRISTOPHER

SKILL 2: COURAGE AND RESILIENCE

There is no doubt that 2020 threw up some huge challenges for leaders. In Australia it started with the most devastating bushfires in history, followed by a pandemic that descended on us within weeks, throwing us into a health and economic crisis at the same time. Every Australian has been touched by these events in some form and many are still grappling with uncertainty and fear.

I reached out to my clients and networks early in the pandemic to offer my help and support as I could see that leaders were struggling with navigating through this mess. We spoke about mental health, stress, rapid change, pivoting, agility, the new normal, working from home, leading remote teams, restructures, and leading through and out of the crisis. Leaders had to build resilience, have tough conversations, and guide their teams and organisations while facing nothing but constant uncertainty.

What I have witnessed has not only surprised me, but has also made me proud of the people I work with. Leaders have truly stepped up and shown real courageous leadership.

Courageous leadership

As previously mentioned, I'm currently working with an organisation in Prague that organises international study tours for university students. I would like to use them now as an example of courageous leadership.

As we all know, the traditional business of travel disintegrated quickly in early 2020, but what this organisation has managed to do, led by their inspiring leader and leadership team, is a prime example of courageous leadership. Within a short amount of time the team identified how to shift their services online and build a whole portfolio of new programs and solutions. Speed, confidence, sensitivity and flexibility are the qualities that made this turnaround successful. It's my model of courageous leadership:

- Speed: make quick decisions with the information you have
- Confidence: be confident about the decisions you have made

- Sensitivity: be sensitive in the way you communicate change and decisions to your teams, clients and stakeholders
- Flexibility: be flexible and adjust as needed

In situations of crisis we don't have the luxury of time for collecting detailed data, lengthy analysis and extensive deliberations. Peter Baines, who leads the charity Hands Across the Water, maintains that a crisis is a critical testing ground for leaders, and that unique challenges require unique solutions. He says: 'Hope is not a plan.'

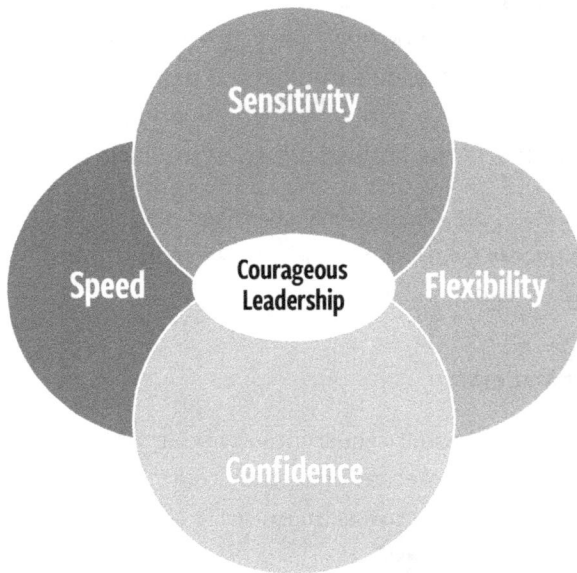

The courageous leadership model

Is courageous decision-making heroic impulsiveness or calculated risk? What comes to mind when you hear the word *courage*? A cartoon version of Super(wo)man saving the world? Someone jumping out of a plane with a parachute strapped to their back? An executive making decisions with authority? Someone who asks you for help because they don't have a solution?

It takes courage to do all of these things. Courage is not limited to heroic actions, despite being associated with them most of the time. It's also about being vulnerable. Courage could be defined as the ability to do something that frightens you. Bravery shows up in all shapes and forms, and has more to do with our behaviour and actions than who we are. Courage can be learned, and is in fact one of the most important leadership skills in the workplace of the 21st century.

We're seeing much flatter organisational structures these days, with a move away from command and control towards collaborative and empowering leadership styles. As I explained with the team-member engagement model, you can see how, with growing engagement, the leadership style moves from directing to influencing. On the level where people lead change and lead the future, the leadership style enables leaders on all levels to feel empowered and in charge. This results in more people in leadership positions being required to make decisions, often bold or risky decisions. For new leaders this can be scary, especially if they lack confidence and decisiveness.

I am currently working with an organisation in the consulting space, and their mostly millennial-aged team has shifted to a purpose-inspired culture. They have an extremely flat hierarchy and complete flexibility when it comes to working from home or in the office. It took them a couple of years to embrace output-driven results, but it has been a successful move. It has hit the bottom line and improved the culture and staff retention.

One of the biggest challenges for some of the new project and people leaders in this company was finding the courage to make decisions, and what was missing was a process. They had to understand that a plan and a process would help them take calculated risks rather than having to rely on heroic impulses.

The Covid-19 pandemic has thrown a blanket of uncertainty over all of us, and I witness more leaders than ever before struggling with decision-making. It's the 'black swans', the unknown unknowns that hold leaders back from making certain decisions for fear of making a wrong one. For example, I talk to many business leaders about how they will organise their workplaces when people start to return to work, and almost all find it hard to decide what the best model is because they have no previous experience or benchmark to fall back on.

> 'A LEADER TAKES PEOPLE WHERE THEY WANT TO GO. A GREAT LEADER TAKES PEOPLE WHERE THEY DON'T NECESSARILY WANT TO GO BUT OUGHT TO BE.'
>
> —ROSALYNN CARTER

In a quest to lead people and businesses into the post-Covid era and the future of work, courageous decision-making might be one of the most powerful leadership skills. Here is my 6-step courageous-decision process (remember, this can be used for any decision, not just important, world-changing ones):

Step 1   *Purpose: Ask yourself why you have to make the decision. What is the purpose of the decision? Does something need fixing? Does something not feel right? Is a move forward needed? Purpose involves getting clarity about the why.*

Step 2   *Assess the situation: Gather all the necessary information, and analyse the project or situation. You also want to weigh up the risks and benefits.*

These two first steps will help you qualify the decision to be made and build the foundations for the plan forward.

Step 3   *Input: Good decisions don't happen in a vacuum. Add to your information gathering by asking people for their feedback, opinions and input. This will inform your decision and also empower your teams as they help you make important decisions. And who's to say you know it all?*

Step 4   *Select the right time: While you want to stay away from heroic impulsiveness, neither do you want to procrastinate unnecessarily. You might want to weigh up: Is this an emergency, or can I take my time for a more deliberate decision? If you feel like you're procrastinating, ask yourself what would happen if you did nothing.*

Step 5   *Confidence: Have the courage to make the decision with all the information at hand. Be confident and believe it's the right decision. Don't start second-guessing yourself the minute you've made the decision; it won't help with your follow-through or with getting buy-in. This is especially important in a crisis.*

Step 6   *Contingency: Always have a plan B. Be confident that you've made the right decision, but keep on gathering information, feedback and experience, and amend as necessary.*

Remember, hope is not a plan. You need to take ownership of the problem, and have the courage to step in and make decisions. Using a process will give you the confidence to do it well.

> 'SUCCESSFUL LEADERS HAVE THE COURAGE TO TAKE ACTION WHILE OTHERS HESITATE.'
>
> —JOHN MAXWELL.

Resilience fast became a buzzword after we were forced to change the way we live our lives in early 2020. Everybody is now talking about the need for building resilience to be able to navigate through these challenging times and the ongoing uncertainty. But resilience is not just a buzzword or fad; it is in fact one of the main skills that leaders need to thrive in a VUCA world. Resilience can be loosely defined as the ability to bounce back from hardship, and in a faster changing and more volatile environment, being resilient will determine how well we recover from setbacks to lead change successfully.

Resilience with a systems view

I explored resilience and resilient leadership early on in the crisis because it impacted me personally, as well as every leader I was working with. For me, it was vital to understand what resilience was, how to build it with practical steps, and how to role model it for others.

I have always considered myself a resilient person. I had put it down to my childhood: losing my father at the age of eight, and being brought up to be independent and solve problems on my own. I was under the impression that you either had resilience or you didn't, and that all resilience was the same and came from the same human resource. So you can imagine my surprise when Covid-19 hit Australia in March 2020 and my emotions and mental health were all over the place. It affected all parts of my life and I wondered what was wrong with me. I was a resilient person, so why couldn't I control my emotions?

What helped me was a renewed view of resilience. My previous view—that you either had resilience or you didn't—no longer applied, and that was why I struggled so much to bounce back. My old way of thinking that it was enough just to believe in myself and use my optimism wasn't working anymore.

If we see resourcefulness through a systems lens, we understand that we have redundant resources to build resilience. Australian researchers Racquel Boyd and Laura Hefer have done extensive research on systemic resilience, and state that we can find redundant resources in the following systems: our personal lives (new habits, sleep and wellness, new skills), social lives (network of friends, family, professional groups), material (technology, financials, extra room at home to use as office) and environmental (nature, space at home to exercise, fresh air). We need to find out in which system we feel depleted, stressed or out of control, and tap into all the different resources to build resilience.[21]

I changed from my single-lens view to a multi-systems approach. My systems are personal life, business, finance and family. When one of my systems is running low, I now find ways to strengthen myself by taking practical steps towards wellbeing. For example, when I feel exhausted and my energy is depleted, a day on the couch and a long sleep-in help me to build resilience. The trick is that I don't feel bad about it; it's my system, my resource. When I started working from home, work took over my whole life and I needed to set boundaries. I started by physically removing my laptop and documents from the dining table at night, and setting a time when I would truly finish work for the day and go for a walk to get separation.

Determine your own systems. Write down your ideas, and evaluate where your cup is full and where it's empty. Filling your finance cup requires different actions to filling your physical-wellbeing cup. This strategy will help you find the right resources and solutions, and also keep your system flexible. Your struggles won't always be the same, so when you feel down go back to your systems and re-evaluate.

What's holding you back from moving forward?

What is often observed when people struggle is that they procrastinate. Dr Adam Fraser calls it the 'happiness movement'. In his work, Fraser says that we hold the view that negative emotions are bad and positive emotions are good. This view has perverted our relationship with struggle. We think we need to feel good or be happy *before* we can take action. Building resilience means 'sitting in discomfort' and acting anyway. People who deal with struggle well manage to sit with discomfort and act without waiting for the situation to change.[22]

This doesn't mean that you can't have a bad day, where you just sit on the couch and indulge in some Netflix. In fact, if you need it you should do it in good conscience, but stay away from thoughts like this: *I'm going to do nothing and wait to feel better so I can move forward*. Sitting in discomfort and taking charge without delay builds resilience. It certainly helped me throughout 2020.

When you feel yourself struggling, create self-awareness of what you're actually thinking. Peel your thoughts like an onion, and validate which stories are true and which stories are made up. I work on this constantly with my coach. She asks me: 'Where is the proof of this actually happening?' She basically calls me on my own prevarication.

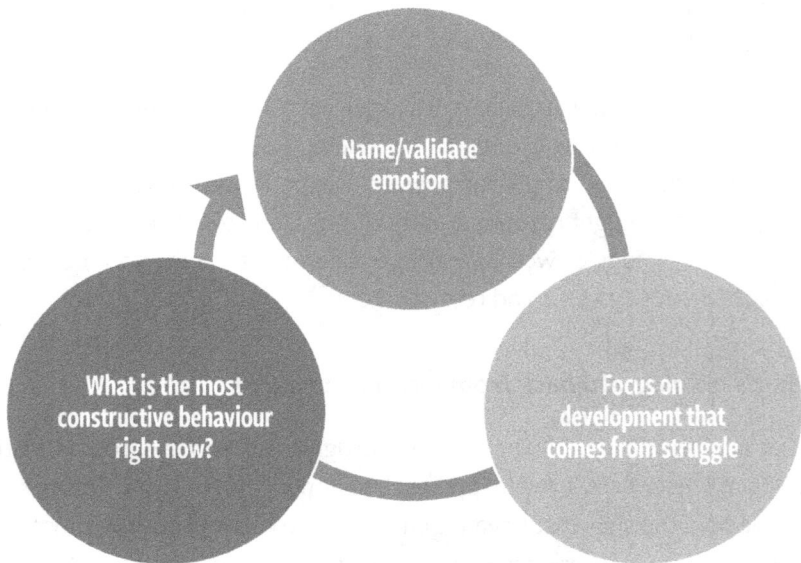

Cycle of resilience building

With change being the only constant in today's world of work and the ongoing Covid-19 crisis, it can feel like we're going through a cycle of constant resilience building. I have been inspired by a series of webinars I have attended throughout the last eighteen months, from which I have accumulated a list of tips:

- Assume the worst and plan for that.
- Create new routines and set boundaries.
- Care about five things (and only five things; Mark Manson).
- Realise how little you need (interesting how we connect to our values right away).
- Do things you enjoy, and find lightness; focus on positive conversations.
- Don't be too hard on yourself. When you're low, be okay with it. Work or relax, and be aware that you feel bad anyway.
- If you want to bounce back, you have to build strength and look after your mental and physical health: sleep, meditate, be okay with how you feel (and action anyway), celebrate progress and give back.

In leadership it's not enough to build resilience for ourselves, we also have a responsibility to lead our teams through change, especially during a crisis. Every change has an impact on us, and we move through something similar to Elizabeth Kubler Ross's five stages of grief.

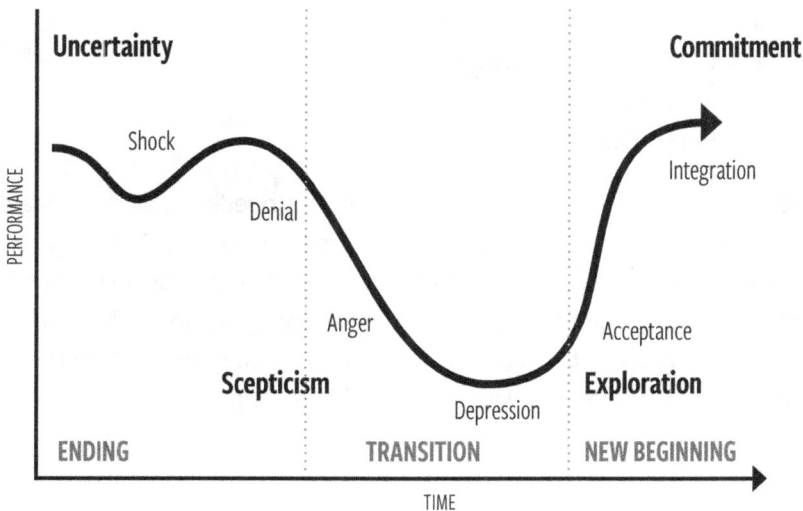

Five stages of grief

The VUCA world, rapid changes through disruption, the shift to remote and hybrid working, social restrictions and restructures—this all means that we're moving through a constant cycle of grief: shock, denial, anger, depression, acceptance, integration. Or, if we overlay the Bridges transition model instead, it would be uncertainty, scepticism, exploration and commitment.

Leaders have to create awareness of these stages and respond with the most helpful communication. Too often I see leaders starting to train staff immediately after a change in positions or projects while their people are still in the anger or depression phase; people need time to accept change and make sense of it. In these phases, they need coaching, transparent communication and collaboration. Training is helpful in the acceptance phase, and even more so in the integration phase.

Where the focus lies in the different stages of grief:

- Shock: compassion
- Denial: empathy
- Anger: compassion, explanation
- Depression: coaching, support
- Acceptance: motivation
- Integration: training and planning

Transparent and consistent communication is needed in all these stages, and of course we can always coach and mentor people. These types of conversations and actions are not absolute; much depends on the specific situation. By understanding early in the grieving (change) process that people need support and empathy before they can be expected to train, plan and collaborate, you will be better able to help them understand and accept the change.

‘RESILIENCE IS NOT ALL OR NOTHING. IT COMES IN AMOUNTS. YOU CAN BE A LITTLE RESILIENT, A LOT RESILIENT, RESILIENT IN SOME SITUATIONS BUT NOT OTHERS. AND, NO MATTER HOW RESILIENT YOU ARE TODAY, YOU CAN BECOME MORE RESILIENT TOMORROW.’

—KAREN REIVICH

SKILL 3: EMOTIONAL INTELLIGENCE

Generally speaking, people don't like to bring emotions into the workplace. Being emotional has long been perceived as a weakness, as is being overly sensitive. But here's the thing. We all have emotions, and they impact us every day in our personal and business lives. Our emotions influence our moods and energy levels, and drive our behaviour and conversations, which means they ultimately impact the people around us as well. Which means that if our emotions drive our behaviour and decision-making, they also impact our performance, productively and unproductively.

‘IN A SENSE WE HAVE TWO BRAINS, TWO MINDS AND TWO DIFFERENT KINDS OF INTELLIGENCE: RATIONAL AND EMOTIONAL.’

—DANIEL GOLEMAN

Emotional intelligence is the ability to perceive, understand, express, reason with and manage emotions within ourselves and others. Applied to leadership, emotional intelligence is about how intelligent we are at using emotions to help drive the best decisions, behaviour and performance. High performance derives directly from the level of emotional intelligence.

In high-performing organisations, people feel significantly more engaged, cared for, valued and motivated. Research has proven that a leader's emotional intelligence is key to their capacity to facilitate emotions in themselves and others. This drives high performance and employee engagement, and a high level of team-member engagement leads to agile teams that lead the future.

If leaders want to succeed in a VUCA world, thrive in hybrid work models and move from a command-and-control leadership style to inspiring their team members, they need to have emotionally intelligent conversations and make emotionally intelligent decisions. To stay relevant in the future of work, leaders need to be able to have difficult conversations, and make courageous decisions and communicate those effectively to their teams, plus manage themselves and others through complexity, stress and high workloads.

The human is at the centre of change

Leaders can't rely on systems and robots to do the work. Machines are there to automate processes. It's up to the human to inspire and empower people. For organisations with remote teams, emotional intelligence has to be at the front and centre of employee interaction, and leaders have to make sure they equip their people with emotional-intelligence skills.

It's more difficult for people to connect and use empathy and emotional reasoning when they're physically disconnected, so that emotional-intelligence muscle needs to be flexed when people are working on virtual platforms. Incidentally, the World Economic Forum ranks emotional intelligence among the top ten skills needed to lead the fourth industrial revolution.[23]

The current global pandemic calls for a focus on emotional intelligence. In times of crisis we increasingly have to deal with emotions like fear, anxiety, depression, frustration and loneliness, which are often heightened during difficult times and can hold us back from moving forward, making decisions and communicating effectively.

The practice of emotional intelligence starts with creating awareness of our emotions, and managing emotions that reflect deliberate behaviour. Some helpful strategies are mindfulness, breathing, keeping a journal, reflecting, discussing, and asking for feedback. When leaders can manage their own emotions, they have the capacity to lead their people and help them with *their* emotions. The skills we develop when we're emotionally intelligent enable us to lead with a clear head and a strong heart.

Emotional intelligence is the way you manage your behaviour

I coached a director of a consulting firm, let's call her Annie, who had been promoted to the role of director twelve months prior to leading a newly formed team of six senior consultants in the banking industry. Two of the team members used to be her peers, based in the same location, while the other four worked regionally in Asia. Two team members were fifteen years older than her.

I was brought in to help Annie improve her team-leadership skills as some of the feedback from her direct reports in a recent review showed that this area needed attention. A three-way conversation with her line manager revealed that he appreciated Annie's expertise and drive, but he believed she needed to bring her team along with her. The team hadn't yet performed at the level the firm had expected. Annie's team members felt that she often made decisions without including them, which left them without autonomy; she didn't cascade important client or department information, which resulted in a lot of rework; and she came across as brash and abrasive in meetings and conversations.

Annie was at first taken aback by her line manager's comments. All she wanted was to succeed in this important, high-pressure role. She had never received feedback like this before. In the past she had always been seen as a collaborative and motivating manager.

When people give us honest feedback, they are showing us how they perceive us. It's their reality and we can't doubt that that's how they experience our behaviour. That was the first revelation for Annie. It's not that her team didn't like her or respect her. They were simply pointing out that what they perceived as her 'unhelpful behaviour' made them feel unappreciated. They also felt they had no decision-making power, and were sometimes a little scared when she burst out in the middle of a meeting.

We unpacked the feedback regarding her 'unhelpful behaviour' and communication style, and I helped Annie unpack the emotions that drove those. As we know, emotions drive behaviour. Annie realised that when she took on the role she had put herself under enormous pressure to prove herself to the executive team. The pressure made her feel anxious, which led her to believe that she had to make all the decisions by herself. She felt too insecure to trust her team.

As the pressure grew, she felt her team members weren't connecting with her and weren't listening, and the only way she thought she could manage the situation was to 'dial it up a notch' and be direct and firm with them. She didn't realise that this came across as putting up armour instead.

Another reason that Annie felt she had to prove herself was that two team members were previously peers and others had had longer tenures. She thought that if she called the shots and was seen as someone who had all the 'necessary intel', her team members would look up to her. Instead, they felt left out, isolated and disempowered.

We took the time for Annie to identify the emotions that were holding her back, and to label them. She felt insecure, anxious, fearful, inferior, inadequate, exposed and worried, all emotions that pointed to Annie feeling scared. She realised that she was scared of failing and had let her emotions manage her instead of her managing her emotions.

We worked together for eight months, and by the end of that time Annie had changed most of her unproductive behaviours to productive behaviours. By identifying and labelling her emotions, she created awareness and could devise strategies to manage herself and inspire her team.

She openly discussed her insights with her team, let her guard down and started creating a collaborative, empowering and trusting team environment. She started to delegate decision-making without back-delegating, increased team-member engagement by letting people talk and come up with solutions, and used feedback loops both ways. The impact after eight months wasn't only a more engaged team; it also resulted in improved performance, with positive client feedback and achieved financial goals.

Applying emotional intelligence to lead people

Leaders who want to impact the people around them and increase engagement need to apply both emotional intelligence and social intelligence, where they tune into other people's emotions. It all starts with us, as leaders, with our self-awareness and ability to manage our own emotions. There is no social intelligence without emotional intelligence.

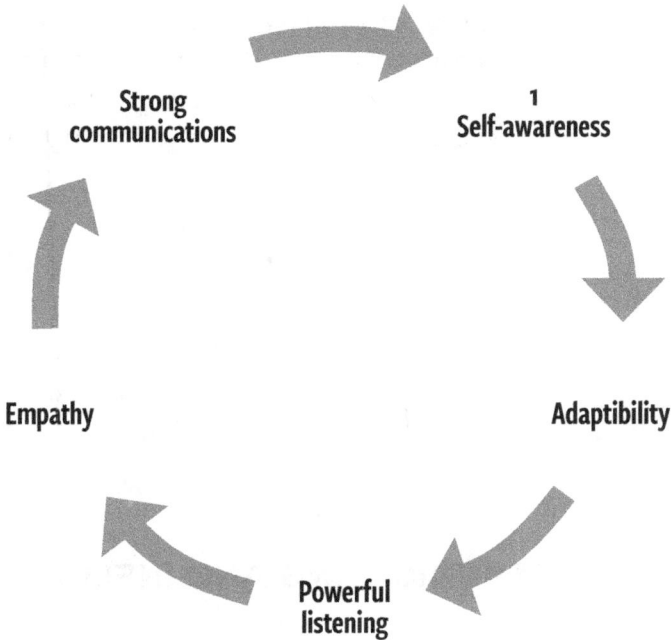

Creating emotional intelligence begins with self-awareness

As leaders, we have to be able to understand another person's point of view: their situation, behaviour and communication style. Their natural behaviour, just like ours, is also driven by emotions, especially when they're under pressure. As leaders, we need the flexibility to adapt and lean in if we want to influence others. There's no point being direct and demanding with someone if they're confused and need more time to digest information.

Powerful listening and applying empathy represent the tuning-in parts of social intelligence. This means taking the time to listen for the other person's emotions and energy, ask open questions, and create space for them to reflect. Being a strong communicator—giving feedback, communicating a tough message, motivating, guiding, mentoring or offering solutions— becomes much easier when we are emotionally and socially intelligent.

The problem is that many leaders are quick to dive right into communication without thinking too much about what's going on for the other person. Leaders can be advice-giving maniacs and we often want to come up with solutions and share our opinions right away. Applying emotional and social intelligence can help to uncover emotions and fears that may be holding someone back from being engaged, and can give you the right levers to empower the people you lead.

'ENGAGING PEOPLE IS MEETING THEIR NEEDS, NOT YOURS.'

—TONY ROBBINS

SKILL 4: COMMUNICATING AND INFLUENCING

You are now moving from Lead Self to Lead Others, where you connect yourself and other people. Connecting well comes from the way you interact with others, communicate with them, and influence their decision-making.

If you want people to make a buying decision, or your board or teams to accept an idea or change, you need to understand the ways in which they will be influenced.

Influencing is not about you; it's about the person or people you want to influence. Understanding different natural behaviour styles simply means understanding why others do what they do; how that may be different from what you do; and how they react, communicate and relate differently (or the same) as you. Uncovering the differences will help you lean into their preferred style of communication and influence them with impact.

Detecting how people behave is a bit like travelling to a foreign country where you simultaneously watch how people behave and discover their culture. And because you want to blend in, you adapt to their way of navigating in the community.

It's similar in business. People have different behaviour styles, meaning they react to events in different ways, and they might express themselves differently to you. For example, when a project deadline is close some people become anxious, or even frantic, while others stay calm and on course. It's all about discovering what your natural style of behaviour is and how you react in certain situations, especially when you're under pressure. Once you've determined this, you can detect what other people's high preferences are.

When people react in unexpected way to situations, or to your communication, try not to take it personally. Instead, understand that's just what people do naturally. You'll remember from the previous section on emotional intelligence that behaviour is driven by emotion. Everyone has their own habitual way of reacting, their own natural behaviour style.

Behaviour is an expression of your personality

I experienced this firsthand when I worked in Japan in 2011. When I arrived, I noticed that people behaved quite differently from those in Hong Kong or Australia. In Japan, I found the people a lot more reserved, very indirect in terms of language, and very modest with body language. Because I'm an enthusiastic and direct communicator with a loud voice and use big hand gestures, my Japanese counterparts in business meetings seemed frightened, staring at me with big eyes and leaning away from me.

Not being able to connect with these prospective clients and business partners meant I had to learn how to hold myself back more, become more reserved, and use a much softer approach. This was necessary so I could win their trust, take away what seemed like their fear of me, and put us more on the same page. I basically adapted my behaviour style to theirs.

I understood that some of the clashes came as a result of cultural differences, but my previous experience in understanding the fundamental difference in different people's behaviour styles and how to influence my teams and clients helped me enormously in becoming successful in the Japanese role and market.

Our world is now more globalised than ever, which means the geographic spread of the talent pool in remote team environments is much wider, and as a result leaders are expected to connect increasingly diverse groups of people. If leaders want to inspire, engage with and empower distributed workforces in flat hierarchies, they need to learn how to influence from a non-leadership position and then teach others to do the same thing.

In a quest to create the next normal, we need others to buy into ideas and bring themselves in as well. A recent *Forbes* article about influencing the future states: 'The traditional top-down decision-making flow of traditional businesses has proven to be more of a roadblock than an enabler for success in today's marketplace. When the competitive edge is about creating the new and carving out unexplored paths, a business needs all ideas on deck.'[24]

I use the DISC diagnostic tool to help people discover their own natural behaviour style. This model has helped millions of people improve their ability to influence others and create more effective relationships at work; in fact, the DISC model is commonly called an 'influencing tool'. William Marston, who published *Emotions of Normal People* in 1928, elaborated on the DISC theory of two axes and four behaviour styles. Walter Vernon Clarke developed the DISC assessment; the modern version looks like this.

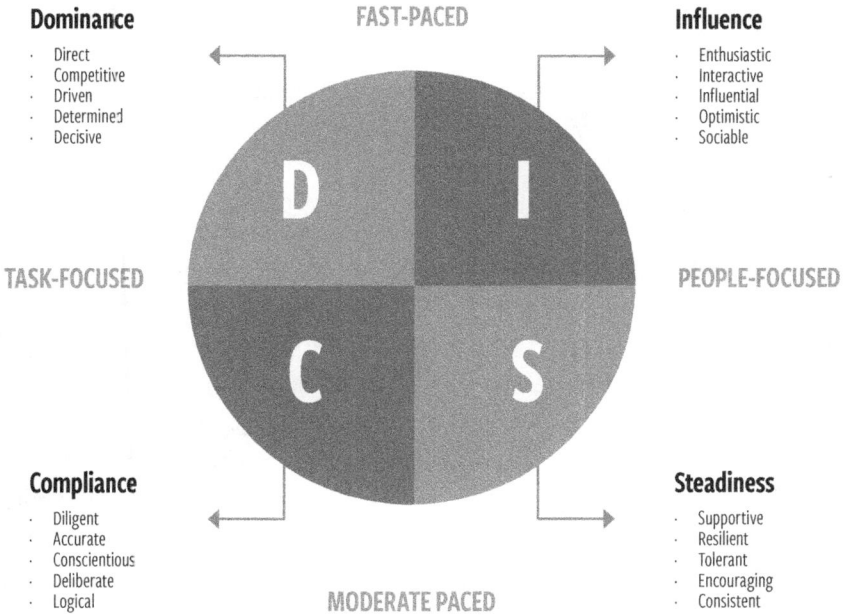

Dominance
- Direct
- Competitive
- Driven
- Determined
- Decisive

FAST-PACED

Influence
- Enthusiastic
- Interactive
- Influential
- Optimistic
- Sociable

TASK-FOCUSED

D   I

C   S

PEOPLE-FOCUSED

Compliance
- Diligent
- Accurate
- Conscientious
- Deliberate
- Logical

MODERATE PACED

Steadiness
- Supportive
- Resilient
- Tolerant
- Encouraging
- Consistent

The DISC model. Source: DISC Flow

The DISC assessment will determine your high preference in one of the quadrants, but remember that we are all shades of all styles. We simply have a high preference, which usually shows up when we're under pressure.

The attributes on the outside describe your natural behaviour style by looking at your preference on two scales: 1) task versus people, and 2) fast paced versus moderate paced.

We find it easier to interact with people who behave similarly to us. They will move at the same pace when it comes to communicating and decision-making, and be similarly influenced by either people or facts and data. We can struggle if we deal with someone who is different from us, especially when they fall into the opposite quadrant.

I worked with a client in Hong Kong a few years ago. His natural behaviour style was steadiness, and he leaned more toward the people side, craving harmony, giving support, being steady, and working well with structure. He was having challenges with his leader, who was on the opposite side of the DISC model and was very direct, fast, abrupt, and always looking for results. When they were both under pressure their individual styles were magnified and their communication wasn't productive. In fact, at one stage my client thought he was about to be fired.

We returned to the DISC model, and as soon as he accepted that it had nothing to do with his leader not liking him, and everything to do with her way of reacting to a stressful situation, he knew what to do. He understood that he had to lean into her behaviour style and deliver solutions rather than problems, give her bullet-point summaries of what was going on, lay out objectives, and be faster with his communication. In other words, the same content but delivered differently so she could understand it in her own natural way. This was a 180-degree turn for him, but he quickly succeeded in handling conversations with her and managed the situation with her effectively.

'THE MOST IMPORTANT THING IN COMMUNICATION IS HEARING WHAT ISN'T SAID.'

—PETER F DRUCKER

To be able to build trust and influence others, we have to detect what their language, communication and behaviour styles are. In order to influence others more significantly, we need to be able to flex into their style so we're on the same level, making it easier for them. We have to be better leaders across *all* styles.

Facilitating team meetings in a virtual world

In this hybrid world, many of us work from home, and I still see many leaders struggling with remote leadership, especially when it comes to running effective team meetings. It's hard enough to keep team meetings engaging and impactful when everyone meets in the same room; working remotely has only added to that challenge. *You're on mute. You just froze. Anyone have any questions?* These are just some of the phrases we have become used to through Zoom meetings. The main challenges we face when we meet virtually are:

- Short attention span: It's harder to keep people focused for long periods of time.
- Multitasking: When people are not engaged they tend to do other things, like answer emails, and on an online platform it's much easier to get away with it.
- Home/work environment: People working from home can get distracted by pets, family, ambient noise.
- Introvert/extrovert: With a lack of presence and body language, these personality traits can become more obvious, with extroverts taking up more airtime and introverts being quieter than usual.
- Zoom fatigue: People are growing tired of constant video-based meetings.

Team leaders need to go back to the drawing board and be intentional about their meetings, starting with planning the meeting, conducting the meeting, and changing the parameters if necessary.

I am currently working with a team leader in the banking industry who managed to reinvent virtual team meetings early on in their work-from-home (WFH) world. Before having any tactical meetings, she called for a virtual meeting with her leaders so they could all come up with their preferred structure and content going forward. This worked well for her and her team because everyone felt empowered to have a say, and they also felt accountable since some of the ideas came from them. The accompanying flexibility and feedback ensured that the meetings were relevant at all times.

They agreed to have a check-in at the beginning of each meeting (now changed to an icebreaker), departmental updates published on OneNote twenty-four hours prior to the meeting, and each team member prepared at least one here-is-how-you-can-help-me item to discuss with the team (brilliant for problem-solving, critical thinking, etc). They take turns taking the minutes and there is a two-minute feedback loop at the end of each meeting. Meetings are capped at forty-five minutes. This team leader has managed to have only twenty percent airtime and acts as a facilitator only; the heavy lifting comes from the team itself.

I have designed six practical steps to make your meetings more effective and keep your team members motivated:

Step 1   *Plan: Take time to plan your meeting, including an anticipated outcome and agenda. Think about timing. Not every meeting needs to be one hour. Consider sending updates and data ahead of time to all team members to digest, and use the meeting time to problem-solve, brainstorm or innovate. Also, involve your team members in the design of the meetings. Ask them what they need to get out of the meeting. Remember, it's as much their meeting as it is yours.*

Step 2   *Instruct: Be specific when sending the calendar invite and content. Send the agenda along with what you expect from everyone during the meeting. Let them know what they need to prepare, read or think about. This will allow you to call on everyone, which will encourage your quieter team members to participate, and airtime will be more balanced. This will also give you opportunities for interventions (e.g. give feedback to people who don't come prepared).*

Step 3   Prepare: Make sure all team members are set up appropriately so they can participate. Use suitable technology and platforms, and offer resources if necessary. Prepare your documents and PowerPoint presentations or slide decks if you're using them. Think of ways in which you can connect with your audience without using data and graphs. For instance, you could tell a business story that relates to the subject of your presentation, or use interactive tools of technology such as the chat function or breakout room with digital communication tools. Write a run sheet for yourself so you stay on track and don't run over time. Send a reminder to team members if necessary.

Step 4   Conduct: Lead by example in making sure you're not distracted. Follow the agenda and honour everyone's time. Consider check-ins at the beginning to get everyone's attention, and also make it personal and fun. Engage with people and use video, camera on or off depending on what is conducive for your team. It can be great for people to see each other, but it can also be draining for those who have lots of virtual meetings. Leave time for Q&A and feedback at the end of the meeting. Ask for feedback on how the team meetings are working for everyone and take suggestions into consideration.

Step 5   Review: Use the feedback and outcomes, and review the meetings. Measure engagement, goals and strategies from the meeting, and overall feedback from team members.

Step 6   Change: Be flexible with your meeting content and purpose, and make changes as you, the team members and the organisation see fit. There might be parts that you have to make mandatory to ensure business outcomes and performance, but you could change the way these are facilitated and presented. Consider getting your team members more involved; put them in charge of conducting part of the meeting and let them determine what should be included. This will result in increased buy-in. Remember, you are the conductor; you don't have to play every instrument.

Virtual presenting: what's different?

For the last year or so much of our business communication has been through screens that show small pictures of people's heads, updates on shared documents, and conversations through chat rooms. And this is not going to change anytime soon. Even when businesses are able to move their workforces back to the office, virtual meetings are here to stay.

I'm having my fair share of experience in communicating with people online. From webinars to online trainings, virtual meetings to coaching sessions, my business runs completely digitally at the moment.

When facilitating or presenting in a room, we have the advantage of using our body language to connect with people and make impact. Content and tone of voice are also important and all three elements need to be congruent, but body language always wins. Showing up virtually requires a different focus in order to present with impact. There are three key areas to consider:

1.   Content: Content is always important, but when presenting online your audience will focus on it even more. At the same time you will have the challenge of keeping people engaged for a long period of time.

      • Send any technical and detailed updates ahead of time so people can get familiar with the content.
      • Share the agenda ahead of time and set expectations so people come prepared.
      • Keep it brief; why not have a 20- or 45-minute meeting?

2.   Present/facilitate: You have to work harder when presenting online due to the lack of real connection with people. Make sure your audience can hear and see you clearly.

      • Sit up straight and breathe: I even facilitate sessions standing up, which helps with energy.

- Ensure you have good light: invest in a ring light that lights up your face but is not distracting.
- Talk to the camera: I have a Post-it note with an arrow on top of my laptop to remind me.
- Use gestures, but keep eye contact.

3. Engage your audience: Engagement means more heavy lifting when done virtually, but is really important. Keep your audience engaged and make them part of your presentation.

- Use available tools like chats, polls, whiteboards and breakout rooms.
- Before you begin your presentation, ask the audience to participate. This should avoid 'crickets' (no reply or reaction at all).
- Speak to people as if they are in the room (*you* versus *you guys out there*).
- PowerPoint presentations provide a service to your audience; they should not be a content crutch. A good rule of thumb is one image, one word, and few animated bullet points.

> '
> WE ARE HARD-WIRED TO ENGAGE WITH THOSE WE TRUST, AND THIS HARD-WIRING HAS LED TO A CONSTANT PUSH FOR GREATER INTERACTION AND CONNECTION ON THE WEB.'
>
> —DAVID AMERLAND

SKILL 5: FEEDBACK AND PRODUCTIVE CONFLICT

Giving effective feedback is a process, just like when you explain to your children that their actions have consequences rather than just telling them to stop their behaviour. The problem with feedback in business is that leaders don't give enough, consistent or effective feedback. Statistics show that over eighty percent of people leave their workplace because of their manager or management, and four out of five employees who receive negative feedback begin job hunting. However, bad feedback is still better than no feedback at all.

> 'FEEDBACK IS THE BREAKFAST OF CHAMPIONS.'
>
> —KEN BLANCHARD

I once worked with a team leader of junior salespeople in the real estate industry. He was new to the role and struggled with giving critical feedback. To him, it felt like a negative conversation and he feared his team members wouldn't like him if he criticised them. Consequently he avoided feedback altogether, which resulted in a very low retention rate in his team, so his manager brought me in to help him.

We worked through a process of demonstrating how he could give feedback effectively: this then helped him lose his fear of what he perceived as criticism and instead see the value in helping his team members improve. People need feedback, both positive and negative, so they can learn what to continue doing and what to stop doing.

SBI feedback model

The SBI feedback model stands for situation, behaviour and impact:

- Situation: Be specific about the situation (when, who, where)
- Behaviour: Describe the behaviour you observed
- Impact: Point out what impact the behaviour had

Using this model will ensure that you give effective and helpful feedback. When you give feedback, make sure you do it right away, that you do it in private and that you use the SBI model.

Start by explaining the situation. Be specific and describe what you see. Explain the behaviour. And make sure that you tell your team member what impact their behaviour has had. That makes it much less personal because you're not attacking the person, you're simply explaining the situation, their behaviour, and the impact of their behaviour. Then you and your team member can work together on a solution. Ask them how they would solve the problem.

Giving feedback often and giving feedback well will help your team members to improve, be happy and stay happy.

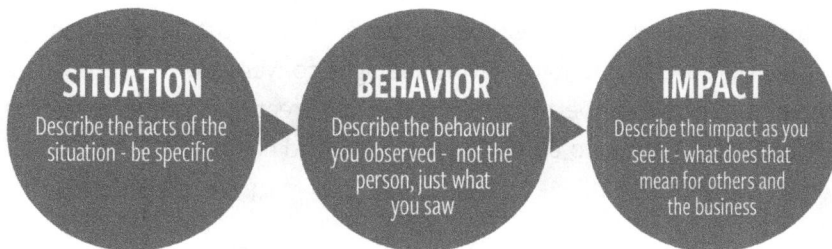

SITUATION
Describe the facts of the situation - be specific

BEHAVIOR
Describe the behaviour you observed - not the person, just what you saw

IMPACT
Describe the impact as you see it - what does that mean for others and the business

The SBI feedback model

Here is an example of the SBI feedback model in action.

Scenario: 'Thomas, in the team meeting this morning (*situation*), I noticed that you interrupted Susan and Mary a number of times (*behaviour*). This resulted in them not bringing themselves in for the rest of the meeting, and in fact they mentioned to me that they felt disrespected and didn't want to join anymore unless this changed (*impact*).'

Follow-on: Use a question (*coaching approach*) or direction (*guiding*) so Thomas can change his behaviour.

A few tips:

- Consistency: Give feedback often and use models like SBI to do it effectively. It will help your team members improve their performance and stay engaged.
- Immediacy: Give feedback directly after a situation or incident, otherwise it won't seem relevant.
- Privacy: Give critical feedback in private, not in front of other people.
- Balance: Bad feedback is just as important as positive feedback, but all feedback should be constructive. Make sure you praise your team members for effort, not ability.

Creating a feedback culture: the two-way road

For me, leadership in organisations comes down to two things: relationships and conversations. When leaders do both—build trusting relationships with people around them by having the right conversation— the positive impact on team members can be substantial. Creating a feedback culture will help your people to be more productive and happier.

> ' IT TAKES HUMILITY TO SEEK FEEDBACK. IT TAKES WISDOM TO UNDERSTAND IT, ANALYZE IT AND APPROPRIATELY ACT ON IT.'
>
> —STEPHEN COVEY

Creating a feedback culture is a two-way street. Give and ask for feedback. You empower your team members when you show them that you are interested in their opinions about the structure of the meetings, and whether or not it is working. It also shows your willingness to listen to feedback and that you're leading by example.

Another important point is that the feedback you get will help to improve your own processes or work. For example, I always ask for feedback after my leadership workshops so I can improve content and the way I facilitate. There are a few simple steps to take in asking for feedback:

- Ask for feedback overtly, being specific about what you want feedback on.
- Thank people for their feedback.
- Return the favour.
- Be objective when receiving feedback.
- Commit to following through on changes you agree to implement.

Creating a feedback culture is more than just adopting a model and giving good feedback. Changing a culture means changing conversations across the board, where people develop the habit of giving and receiving feedback consistently. It will become part of your company's DNA. There are two other areas you could consider.

First, start at the top. It has to be clear to people that feedback is a positive influencing tool and will improve processes and behaviour. I suggest you start at the top of your team or organisation, where feedback is role-modelled consistently. People need to feel that feedback is a normal part of day-to-day conversations among *all* team members. Ensure that people are trained (SBI model) and that feedback is part of 360 reviews. If it is used to demote people, trust will be lost. Use balanced feedback.

Second, consider feedback DNA. Feedback culture goes beyond following a process. It's not just about telling someone to do or not do something; it's more to do with the way you go about it. In a *Harvard Business Review* article, Ed Batista shared four crucial areas of creating a feedback culture: safety and trust, balance, normalcy and personal accountability.[25]

The diagram below illustrates the elements that make for a successful feedback culture.

Creating a feedback-rich culture takes time and will involve everyone in your organisation. A good start is to teach your managers/leaders to use the SBI model and encourage them to use consistent feedback.

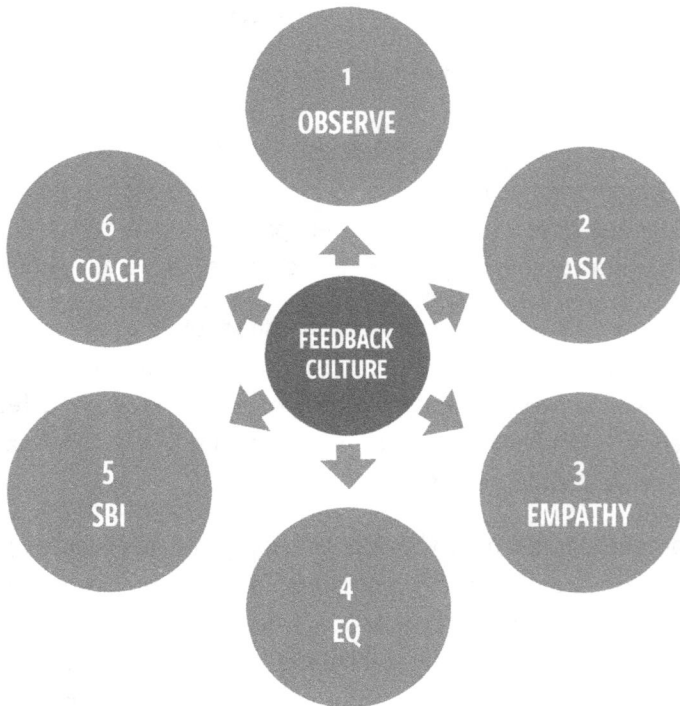

Successful feedback culture

Productive conflict

Do you feel like you're working in a team where everyone gets along but real issues are being avoided? Is your manager someone who makes all the decisions and doesn't ask for input? Do you feel uneasy voicing your concerns or presenting your ideas to groups of people in fear of rejection? Do you, as a leader, avoid conflict to create harmony?

> IN GREAT TEAMS, CONFLICT BECOMES PRODUCTIVE. THE FREE FLOW OF CONFLICTING IDEAS IS CRITICAL FOR CREATIVE THINKING, FOR DISCOVERING NEW SOLUTIONS NO ONE INDIVIDUAL WOULD HAVE COME TO ON HIS OWN.'
>
> —PETER SENGE

All of these experiences are not uncommon, and I observe them again and again when working with leaders and intact teams. The word *conflict* has a negative connotation. A large number of leaders avoid conflict altogether, or they don't know how to create a culture that is conducive to people being open to debate and brainstorming; however, encouraging productive (constructive) conflict is one of the most important leadership skills for team leaders and executives.

In a *Forbes* article, Roger Dean Duncan says: 'I've often told my clients that if you have ten people at a table and they agree on every single issue, you no doubt have the wrong ten people. Conflict is not inherently bad. Conflict is not some noxious weed that needs to be eradicated from the organisational garden. In fact, conflict—when it's handled appropriately—can lead to breakthrough solutions.'[26]

To lead the future and mobilise your teams, you need everyone to bring ideas to the table. Everyone needs to discuss them, evaluate them and pressure-test them, or toss them out and invite new ideas. Be open and critical, and remember that *nice* doesn't equal *effective*. Create environments with trust and engagement so conflict becomes productive. Build the foundations and culture first, otherwise there will be conflict without it being productive.

A few years ago I worked for a Hong Kong-based company as a sales director. On the surface, the CEO promoted productive conflict by telling us he wanted to hear our ideas, saying he was open and eager to learn from everyone. We had daily executive meetings where we discussed different areas of the business, but to me they never felt like open and honest conversations. The fundamental problem was that there was no trust or psychological safety to engage in conflict: ideas were shut down, certain topics were taken offline quickly, there was lots of talking behind someone's back if they challenged the status quo, and so on. Favouritism and gossip thrived, and people who told the boss what he wanted to hear were promoted. Needless to say, I left the company—and so did everyone else.

Productive conflict doesn't stand on its own, and it won't happen without a level of trust and psychological safety. If people fear that their actions might have negative consequences, they will put on their armour and disengage. All you will get is people being careful about what they say and contribute.

When people don't feel safe to speak up, bring forward their own ideas or challenge the status quo, they will not engage in productive debate. Once you build a culture where people feel safe to be vulnerable, be themselves, be creative and speak up, you can encourage productive conflict. Just as emotional intelligence has a direct link to performance, productive conflict has a direct impact on team performance.

> ' A WILLINGNESS TO TRUST AND OPENLY LISTEN TO ALTERNATIVE IDEAS AND VIEWS IS ESSENTIAL FOR COLLABORATION TO BE SUCCESSFUL.'
>
> —DALE EILERMAN

Here is my model for leaders who are looking for growth and team performance.

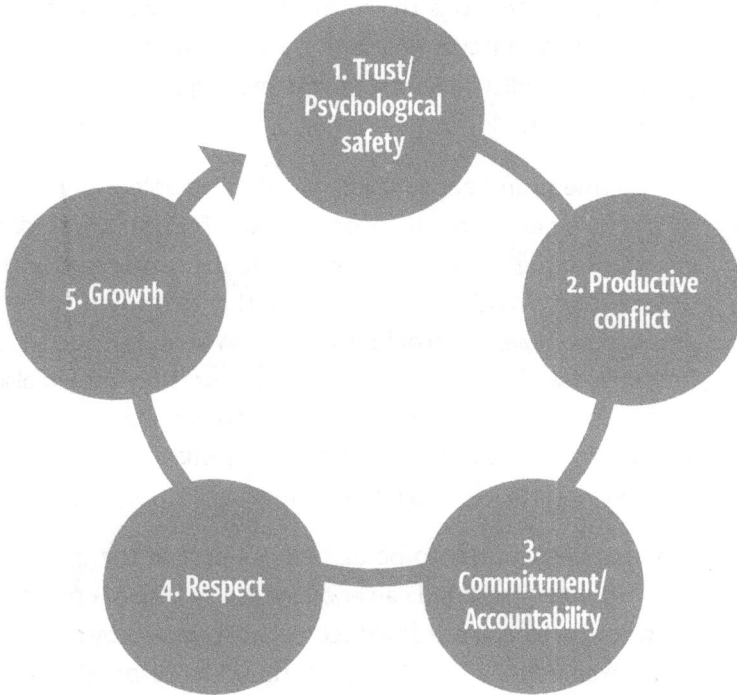

Model for increasing team performance

- Trust and psychological safety: Start by demonstrating trust behaviours like vulnerability, asking for help, letting everyone speak, listening, and constructive feedback. Building trust is all about showing people that you have their back, that you personally care, and that you can connect and communicate in a meaningful way.

  If you discover a lack of trust within your team, work on team communication and teach skills like giving and receiving feedback, coaching skills, radical candour and so on. Create a culture where team members feel safe to ask questions, ask for help and voice ideas, no matter how left of centre they may be. Make it safe for people to say: *I don't agree with you, but I appreciate your point of view.*

- Productive conflict: Once you have created openness and a level of trust, you can encourage productive conflict. Make brainstorming and feedback sessions the norm. Make sure your teams work on projects and issues that are in their control. You can bring productive conflict into most of your meetings and conversations; make it a habit.

- Commitment and accountability: When people are in charge, or are being asked for their opinion and feel empowered, they will show a higher level of commitment to the team and the organisation. What's important here is that all team members are held accountable, not only for their performance but also for their mistakes, and their good and bad behaviour. They should also be recognised for their achievements. There is nothing more deflating than overcoming a challenge or delivering amazing results without receiving an iota of recognition or feedback.

- Respect: Respect has to be earned. It's part of the cycle. Once you've created trust and can encourage a culture of constructive conflict where people are held accountable, respect by staff, clients and stakeholders will increase. There will be respect for leaders doing the right thing and encouraging everyone actively to be part of the organisation.

- Growth: This will look different for everyone, depending on what growth means to the individual. Growth will happen if you start with trust. If you experience challenges like underperformance, lack of productivity or collaboration, and possibly a decrease in sales, go back in the circle and find out where your team is stuck. Chances are you might have to work on increasing trust again.

Psychological safety for high-performance teams

Let's shine a light on psychological safety. Have you ever worked in an environment where you or others were held back from sharing ideas, speaking up when you could clearly see things were going wrong, admitting mistakes, or asking questions? If so, you likely experienced a lack of psychological safety.

In a culture where there is a lack of psychological safety, people are often afraid to present ideas or challenge the status quo. In situations where it's about life or death, for instance in an operating theatre or on an aircraft, this can be detrimental to people's safety. In the corporate world it can impact the team's performance and have a significant influence on a business's financial success.

> LOW LEVELS OF PSYCHOLOGICAL SAFETY CAN CREATE A CULTURE OF SILENCE. THEY CAN ALSO CREATE A CASSANDRA CULTURE—AN ENVIRONMENT IN WHICH SPEAKING UP IS BELITTLED AND WARNINGS GO UNHEEDED.'
>
> —AMY C EDMONDSON

In my earlier story about the real estate company I worked for in Asia, the culture was riddled with behaviours like bullying, gossiping and unhealthy competition for being popular. It truly was a Cassandra culture. And while it was the most extreme toxic culture I have ever worked in or seen again, I know that elements of a lack of psychological safety exist in many teams and organisations.

In her book *The Fearless Organization,* Amy C Edmondson explains that it's human instinct to 'fit in and go along'. Our job as leaders is to create psychological safety so our people feel safe to bring themselves in, no matter how crazy they think an idea might be, and to ask questions without fear of being laughed at. This is how teams stay innovative.

Edmondson describes psychological safety as the belief that 'one will not be punished or humiliated for speaking up with ideas, questions,

---

concerns or mistakes'. However, a recent Gallup report shows that only three in ten workers strongly agree that their opinions seem to count at work. Creating psychological safety has to be uppermost in every leader's agenda.

> '
> PSYCHOLOGICAL SAFETY IS NOT A PERK; IT'S ESSENTIAL TO PRODUCING HIGH PERFORMANCE IN A VUCA WORLD.'
>
> —AMY C EDMONDSON

A good place to start is by building trust in order to engage productive conflict. It's important to understand that psychological safety doesn't equal trust. Trust is giving another person the benefit of the doubt and making them believe they are doing the right thing. Psychological safety relates to whether others will give *you* the benefit of the doubt. Psychological safety is not the only thing needed to achieve high performance, but it is foundational and a prerequisite to innovation, collaboration, staying flexible, and being ahead of the game.

Leaders may not be able to make their workplaces completely fearless, but they should do their best to create a high level of psychological safety, not just for the sake of performance but also to protect team members and clients.

Psychological safety, as with most things, starts with leaders. The following diagram illustrates my seven steps for creating a psychologically safe culture.

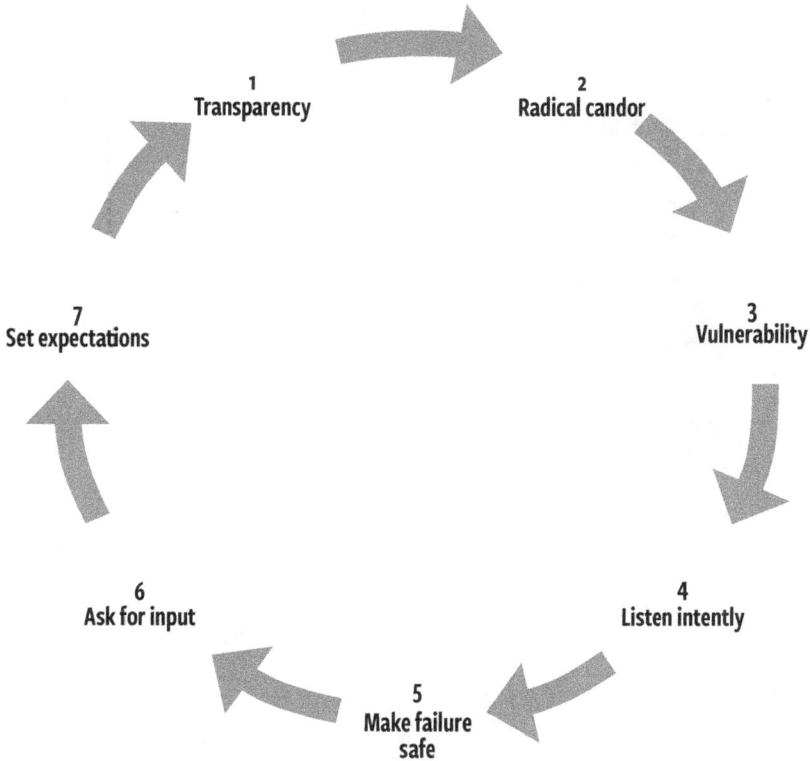

Creating psychological safety

Step 1   Transparency: It's not just about transparent information flow;
          it's about transparent team communication. Don't allow people
          to talk behind each other's backs. Gossip can be detrimental to
          creating psychological safety. Call it out and lead by example. If
          someone is not in the room, they won't be talked about. The same
          goes for copying (or blind copying) people into communications.
          Agree on what transparency means to your team.

Step 2   Radical candour: If you want candid conversations you must ensure
          that people care personally for each other. 'Radical candour', a
          term coined by Kim Scott, explains how both personal care and
          direct challenges are important for candour to work. Build trust

first, and then encourage people to challenge ideas, decisions and plans.

Step 3   *Vulnerability: Be someone who doesn't know it all. The easiest way to take away the fear people may have about speaking up is for you to ask questions. Say 'I don't know' and admit when you have failed or made a mistake. Lead by example and show vulnerability without losing your confidence.*

Step 4   *Listen intently: Don't just listen to reply; instead, listen to understand. Take the time to listen, pause, ask clarifying questions and make notes. And remember that body language is just as important as spoken language.*

Step 5   *Make failure safe: When things go wrong, people make mistakes or projects fall over, so speak openly about this with your team. Look at things from all angles, but focus on what everyone has learned from it. Some companies even reward failure.*

Step 6   *Ask for input: Always. But be specific about what you expect from the team. When you brainstorm, make sure that you record all ideas; don't dismiss any, no matter what they are. If you have team members with a different cultural background that makes it harder for them to come forward, make sure they have all the information they need ahead of time, so they are not caught out in the moment.*

Step 7   *Set expectations: If you want people to come up with ideas, challenge the status quo and meet expectations, they need to know what the purpose is. Set expectations clearly on what is expected, by when, and what it should look like. Don't be vague and leave people to guess. Encourage people to think outside the box. Additional information and parameters will make everyone feel comfortable, and encouragement to venture outside the comfort zone will move the needle.*

SKILL 6: LEADING IN A HYBRID WORLD

What a year last week has been. Have your workweeks been like this, when you feel like a whole year has been crammed into one week? You wake up on Monday morning and next thing you know it's seven pm on Friday. The years 2020 and 2021 have been a rollercoaster; time has flown by and so much has changed. The corporate world has had to move into working from home, and lockdowns have been a learning curve for both businesses and employees. As we're slowly returning to our offices, one thing is clear: we're not going back to the way things were.

> '
> EVEN WHEN I WORKED IN AN OFFICE, I WOULD OFTEN BRING WORK HOME WITH ME. WHEN I STARTED WORKING REMOTELY, IT WAS JUST A RECIPE FOR DISASTER. OVER TIME, I'VE FOUND TWO THINGS TO BE VERY IMPORTANT. THIS IS A BIT CLICHÉ AND EVERYBODY SAYS THIS BUT IT'S REALLY TRUE: REST IS VERY IMPORTANT. AND TIME OFF IS VERY IMPORTANT.'
>
> —GONCALO SILVA

We need to refocus on employee engagement and wellbeing. The future of work, accelerated by the pandemic, has changed our entire leadership landscape, and the way we work together and communicate with each other. It has impacted supply chains, talent acquisition, the solving of problems and collaboration. Hybrid and remote working are not fads; they are our new canvass, and it's up to us to decide what we want the new picture of leadership to look like.

The future is hybrid

What is a hybrid workplace? It's where employees work from the office some days and remotely on others. Or where an organisation's workforce is divided between those who work in the office and those who continue to work from home. As we move into this hybrid mode of working, businesses need to rethink how they organise work, and leaders need to change their approach to how they lead their teams. The hybrid mode has changed how people work with each other being (partially, at least); being physically disconnected impacts work culture.

Some of the challenges we're seeing are disconnection, loneliness, lack of motivation, lack of productivity, or increased productivity but at the cost of people's mental health. I hear about lack of trust, overwhelm and fear of the ongoing uncertainty in the world. Everyone is experiencing this transition in unique ways. We all have our own fears and motivators, and are dealing with different personal situations.

The question I get asked most often by leaders facing the hybrid world is: *How do I keep my team engaged?* Engagement is about the connection someone has with their workplace and what they give back. When engagement is high we see happiness and satisfaction, retention and loyalty, productivity and creativity, and satisfied and loyal customers.

We know that high team-member engagement has been identified as the main driver of performance. It's evident that it's become a lot more challenging to maintain engagement when we're not all in the same space at the same time. We have to focus on our engagement strategies to keep people motivated and engaged, even when they're working from their dining tables.

I have created a model with seven steps to help leaders focus on the right strategies in order to increase engagement in their organisations.

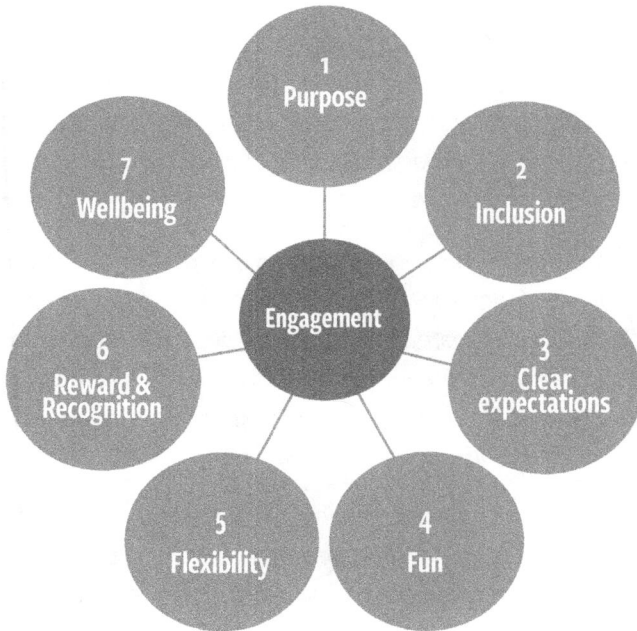

Increasing engagement in organisations

Step 1   Purpose: Re-evaluate your organisation's core values and purpose.
         Are they still in line with what you stand for or have they shifted?
         Look beyond the organisation's purpose and communicate how your
         employees contribute to it. Connect roles to purpose. Encourage
         employees to examine and possibly reconsider how their role ties
         into the greater organisation, but remember that it's the company's
         responsibility to make this connection crystal clear.

Step 2   Inclusion: If your teams are physically disconnected, focus on
         the inclusion of all team members. It can be too easy to forget
         about those quieter introverts who seem happy to work in silos.
         Reach out to those people more often. Be inclusive in your
         meetings and set clear agendas so you can call on everyone
         and give equal airtime to all.

Step 3   *Clear expectations: Be clear about what is expected of people. Again, if people are physically disconnected it can be hard to check in them and throw a quick question across the office. Setting clear expectations and asking for accountability is more important than ever in the current working environment. Also be clear about how the new office and people structure will work.*

Step 4   *Fun: While we are going through one of the toughest phases of our lives, don't forget to keep it light and have some fun. Use fun icebreakers, create time for casual, positive chats, and encourage social times with Zoom drinks or online trivia games. Don't make these activities mandatory; you might find that people still want to connect on a personal, casual level.*

Step 5   *Flexibility: Things are changing faster than ever before. Have an agile mindset and be flexible with regard to changing things when they don't serve you and your team anymore. Your people will also ask you for flexibility going into hybrid mode. Working together on solutions that work for both the individual and the organisation is key to success.*

Step 6   *Reward and recognition: To keep your people motivated, consider introducing reward-and-recognition activities. Remember that recognition is intangible (shout-outs by you and peers, value champions) and reward is tangible (gifts, vouchers, time off). The key to implementing this successfully is acknowledging that rewards and recognition have to be earned, there has to be a personal value, it has to be timely, and it shouldn't be confused with remuneration. Make rewards visible and use social media to track achievements and peer shout-outs, and make announcements.*

Step 7   *Wellbeing: Introduce wellbeing programs. Social distancing has been a new experience, which has forced employers to look closely at how they can help their employees overcome a sense of isolation. Encourage work-life balance and help your employees set boundaries and implement healthy habits. Train your leaders to look out for signs of mental-health issues and have the appropriate conversations. Your aim is not to solve the issues but to refer those employees to the right health professionals if necessary.*

Increasing engagement and wellbeing will help to shift you and your teams into a new world of work while staying happy and productive. Fostering an inclusive team culture where people feel motivated, stay focused and work with integrity is hard enough for leaders to maintain in normal situations, but it's especially challenging in an environment where the only constant is change. We're facing long periods of uncertainty, we're moving into a hybrid world where many people work from home, and we're all connected virtually.

Our workplaces are shifting, and people are asking for more flexibility. A survey by Hays states: 'Variations in employee circumstances, preferences or requirements within the same workforce could lead to the rise of hybrid teams, which are teams in which some members work in the one co-located workplace while others work remotely. So, each day at your workplace could look very different, with part of your team coming into the office on some days, and others staying at home. This is an entirely new challenge for most leaders, so it's important to think now about how you might best lead your newly hybrid team in the not-too-distant future.'[27]

One of my clients from a global insurance company reported that the organisation has partly returned to their central head office in the CBD of Melbourne, with an allowance of days and a maximum number of team members in the office on each day. She said it was nice to have face-to-face catch-ups and coffees, but on days where half the team was in the office, they all ended up in separate spaces and used Zoom to dial in to team meetings. To my client it felt just like working from home during lockdown.

Many leaders are facing similar challenges as office availability becomes limited, space requires pre-booking, and team members have different priorities. Often, hybrid still means remote. The feedback I get from leaders is that innovation and problem-solving usually happen organically when everyone is in the same space with easy access to each other. We know this is a much tougher challenge in a remote environment, and leaders and teams now need to have a structured organic approach for these team sessions.

Let's look back to when many of us were working from home. The challenges our teams experienced were disconnection, loneliness, lack of accountability, Zoom fatigue, lack of boundaries, lack of cohesion, lack of productivity, or an increase of productivity but at a cost.

In remote collaboration, we experience three kinds of distance: physical (place and time), operational (team size, bandwidth and skill levels) and affinity (values, trust, interdependency). We have to consider all three of these distance challenges, even in a hybrid world, to lead our teams into the next normal.

Flexibility and agility by leaders are key. The foundations of leading a team haven't changed, but leaders need to think on their feet and adapt to the new style of hybrid workplaces. Being out of the office means people miss the social connection with others, which means that motivation decreases, fear increases, and many team members feel lost.

Great leadership starts with leaders who, in a hybrid world, need to adapt and possibly change their mindset:

- Assume everyone does their best
- Trust that people will deliver
- Don't assume that everyone's experience of working from home is the same; allow for individual challenges
- Allow equal time for yourself and others
- Fill up your cup; look after your own physical and mental health

Effective leadership in a hybrid world

There are several strategies for leading teams effectively in a hybrid world. Begin by leveraging technology and resourcing your team. Every remote role depends on technology first, and anything that gets in the way of that will only set back your productivity. Budget for updated, reliable technology. Nothing will kill your team's motivation faster than a laptop crashing or slow programs that trudge through daily tasks. Make sure your team members have the resources to deliver when working remotely.

Moving into hybrid workspaces means that some of your team will be in the office when others are at home, so there will be company rules and safety measures to consider as well. Be organised and informed, and ask your team members what they need to achieve their goals. Do they need technology, time, software, skills, information or mentoring?

Be flexible and adaptable

Adaptability is one of the main skills leaders need when moving into a hybrid world. This is new for all of us and it will take some getting used to. Keep considering people's personal situations, but also get commitment from your teams to maximise face-to-face and online time together.

Ask questions: *What do we need to achieve together? What's the best way for us to get there?* Change has been rapid and constant in the last few months, and I don't foresee it being very different in the near future. Foreseeing change and leading change effectively in collaboration with your teams will be the main challenge, but it all presents opportunities for leaders.

Develop a communication strategy

As most leading will still be carried out remotely, revisit your communication strategy. Use face-to-face time in the office for informal chats, coaching, social events, innovation and solving problems. With a lack of organic communication in a hybrid environment you have to plan and structure your team communication, and seek consensus and commitment from everyone. This may sound tedious, but it is necessary.

After the initial 'over-communication is the new black' back in March 2020, be responsive and intentional with your communication channels. Not every email has to be a Zoom call. Consider Slack, Whatsapp or Messenger for brief messages, and create and join groups. But don't overwhelm people, and avoid sending messages in the middle of the night. The key is to be transparent and agree on how everyone will communicate. Regularly review how it's working, ask for feedback, and make changes if necessary. Have more regular one-to-ones, but don't always use video. Actively reach out to your introverts, but don't expect them to join all the social activities. Be more coach-like and ask questions to find out how your people are doing and where they need help.

Get buy-in from your teams and co-create

The easiest way to get buy-in from your people is to ask them what they need and how they want to work. That doesn't mean you have to respond to their every whim, or disregard organisational goals. It's about establishing processes together that work for everyone, negotiating compromises equally, and empowering your teams to achieve goals in their own way.

Consider all forms of touch points, like hangouts, team meetings, pair buddies and one-to-ones. Get everyone to agree with your hybrid work-and-communication structure, and encourage feedback with the flexibility to amend as needed. Use technology and platforms well. Involve your teams and let them come up with ideas about which channels to use. Do mini hackathons, or run team challenges to maintain motivation and be productive. Have structures in place for reward and recognition, such as shout-outs and physical rewards.

Set clear expectations, give feedback, and offer solutions

The way everyone works has changed so be very clear about what is expected. It could be about working hours, or outcomes, or any number of other issues. No matter what it is, discuss expectations in detail and put them in writing, seek common ground and be open to questions.

Don't stop there. Check that everyone has the skills and resources to meet expectations and provide your people with what they need to set them up for success. Then check in regularly and give feedback. Make feedback a habit; ask for and give feedback in every session. That way you can gauge what works and what doesn't.

Manage accomplishments, not activity

Trust your teams and focus on output, not activity. All too often lately I've been hearing leaders say that they can't trust their team members because they can't see them. You have to assume positive intent from your people. Remember to set clear expectations and get buy-in; this will build trust automatically. If your teams focus on outcome, the emphasis will shift to productivity and delivery rather than what they're doing all day. Keep up your check-ins and feedback, but avoid micromanaging.

Celebrate successes and progress

Nothing motivates people more than celebrating wins. In the absence of office high-fives, consider introducing recognition-and-reward programs. Make them public for peer shout-outs and incentives, and use your internal tech platform (ask your Gen Z's if you're not sure how it works). Have regular check-ins with your teams and get everyone to share a success story in every meeting.

The key is consistency. If you're dealing with people who live in countries that are experiencing lockdowns, ask how they're feeling on a scale of one to ten. Ask them to explain why they chose the number they did. It's about responding to the situation you and your team are in, and tailoring communication in the service of your people.

As the world around us changes, leaders also have to change. What worked last month might not work now. Checking in with your teams, asking for feedback, and recreating the hybrid workplace over and over again will mean you stay at the top of your game and keep your remote teams motivated and focused.

Wellbeing at work

Leaders often ask me how they can look after their people's wellbeing at work. With lockdowns imposed at some stage everywhere in the world during 2020 and 2021, organisations navigated the challenges of entire workforces being remote for the first time. Looking after employees' mental health fast became a priority. It doesn't matter if you've just gone into your second lockdown or are already moving into a hybrid model: where remote and onsite working are combined, mental and physical wellbeing of your people should remain a priority. Wellbeing at work is a priority that's here to stay.

In the European autumn of 2020 I worked with a client in the UK whose organisation had just gone into a second lockdown. The client knew it was going to be a tough winter for their people. Being physically disconnected and experiencing loneliness, overwhelm, uncertainty and burnout amounted to what has been called the 'second pandemic'.

This client had returned to daily check-ins with 'wellbeing moments', where employees were encouraged to talk about how they were feeling and why. It enabled open conversations that were not always easy to have, although it is generally accepted that talking about mental health and acknowledging emotions and labelling feelings helps alleviate difficult emotions, creates empathy and helps open up communication channels.

In a recent *Forbes* article, Tracy Brower shares why wellbeing is so important to the future of work: 'Wellness and wellbeing have been on the radar screen for a long time and it's a rare business leader who couldn't recite why they are important. But a year later—after the beginning of the pandemic—there have been big changes to the work we do and how we do it. As a result, leaders and companies must think in new ways and implement expanded and creative solutions to support wellbeing for the future of work.'[28]

The diagram below shows the six strategies that help to prioritise wellbeing and mental health at work.

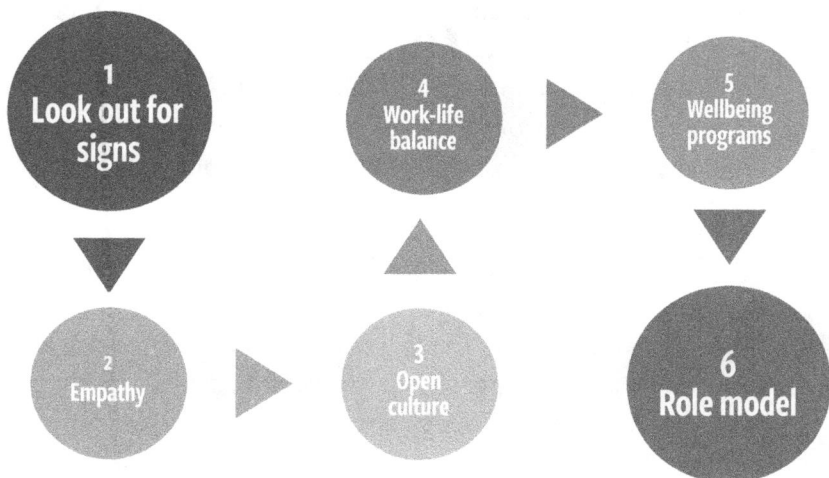

Creating wellbeing at work

- Look for signs: Leading a hybrid workforce requires a different leadership style, where we have to supercharge our social-intelligence skills and tune into our people. Being physically disconnected makes it much harder to identify the signs that someone is struggling. Common signs to watch out for are a change in mood or behaviour, feelings of anxiety or overwhelm, indications of withdrawal from their work, and a lack of motivation or focus.

  Also important are the ways in which people interact with each other, and react to situations and conflict. It is much harder to make these observations through a Zoom screen, so we need to create time and space to ask the right questions, and find opportunities to identify the warning signs.

- Empathy and support: Many people say that we are all in the same boat, but that's not true. We're all facing a similar storm, but our vessels look vastly different. We need to understand that everyone's experiences and personal situations are different. What we're feeling or fearing is different from another person's experience. When your people talk about how they're feeling, make sure they know that whatever that is, it's okay. There should be no comparisons or judgement. Ask what support they need to improve their wellbeing and act on that. It could be anything from flexible work hours to equipment to a certain structure for communication.

- Open culture: Create a culture where it's okay to talk about mental health. Normalise the conversation, because talking about mental health at work can increase trust between co-workers, provide a safe space for those who are struggling in silence, and create a positive and open culture where employees feel that they can bring their full selves to work. Open a two-way dialogue and create a space for people to raise their concerns and be vulnerable. This will help you gain a valuable understanding of their unique situations.

- Work-life balance: Encourage positive work-life balance. When people work from home, their work life and personal life happen in the same space. This can lead to increased levels of stress and workload. Encourage your employees to switch off at a certain time so they can enjoy family and leisure time. If you're receiving emails from them late at night, raise this with them.

  Encourage people to take their holidays, even if there are travel restrictions. Increase flexibility in a way that suits people's family life but also works for the organisation. Often you can find middle ground, but first you need to have the conversation.

- Wellbeing programs: The focus on mental health, and the introduction of or boost of wellbeing programs has increased during the pandemic, yet the number of people rating their mental health as positive is still down compared to before the pandemic. This is a sure sign that the focus has to stay on organisations. There are a number of things organisations can do, including social (online) events, health moments and check-ins, virtual group exercises, resources on mental health, community comms channels, recognition-and-reward programs, and celebrations. Check in with your head office, and let your teams know what's on offer and encourage participation.

- Role-model: Show your people that you are vulnerable by talking about your own mental health. A good way to check in with people is to do a stand-up. Get everyone to talk about how they're feeling on a scale from one to ten, starting with you. Ask people to explain why they chose a particular number; this will encourage them to be specific about what's going on with them.

Role-model work-life balance and stay away from sending emails in the middle of the night. Take part in wellbeing and community events. No matter what you choose to do, remember that people are looking to you to find direction and empathy. Have the tough conversation; ask your people how they are feeling and then provide support.

> SIXTY PERCENT OF WORKERS SURVEYED SAID IF THEIR EMPLOYER TOOK ACTION TO SUPPORT THE MENTAL WELLBEING OF ALL STAFF, THEY WOULD FEEL MORE LOYAL, MOTIVATED, COMMITTED AND BE LIKELY TO RECOMMEND THEIR WORKPLACE AS A GOOD PLACE TO WORK.'
>
> —PAUL FARMER

SKILL 7: AGILITY AND CHANGE MANAGEMENT

You might hear people say 'We're working agile' or 'We're applying agile at our organisation'. I've even been asked if I can facilitate agile workshops, and work within a company's agile methodology. At first, although I had a vague idea of what agile was, I wasn't sure how it connected to leaders specifically or to my practice. My guess is that a lot of people have the same fuzzy understanding of the word used in a business context.

Agility starts with an agile mindset. Originally, the term referred to software development methodologies centred on the idea of iterative development (sprints), where requirements and solutions evolve through collaboration between self-organising, cross-functional teams and their customers. Agile has now evolved into frameworks that enable people to lead change, and adapt products, services and processes quickly and with a high amount of flexibility in every part of an organisation.

Although agile starts with mindset, it is actually challenging to define. Many leaders and organisations use the terms 'agile' or 'agile mindset' without really knowing what they mean. Susan Macintosh explains it well: 'An agile mindset is the set of attitudes supporting an agile working environment. These include respect, collaboration, improvement and learning cycles, pride in ownership, focus on delivering value, and the ability to adapt to change. This mindset is necessary to cultivate high-performing teams, who in turn deliver amazing value for their customers.'[29]

Agility is important for the future of work. In a recent Gallup report, Ghassan Khoury and Mari Semykoz state: 'Changes wrought by digital technologies and the globalisation of markets have come at a breakneck pace in the past decade, forcing businesses to adapt or be swept aside. "Disruptor" companies have rewritten the rules in major industries like entertainment, transportation and hospitality and are transforming customer relationships in many others, from insurance to apparel. It's not surprising, then, that "agility" has become a commonly cited business imperative in recent years.'

I have taken all my research and created a landscape model to make it easier to understand what an agile mindset looks like for me as an individual, and also for teams and organisations. Although it doesn't reflect the agile methodology exactly, it has elements of it.

YOU

INDIVIDUAL

- Self-awareness of ambi-dextrous thinking
- Continuous curiosity, experimenting & learning
- Embrace critical thinking techniques
- Ask for feedback & input
- Reflect & learn from mistakes & failures
- Be humble & hold self accountable

YOU AND
YOUR CLIENT

- Understand your customers & be responsive to their needs
- Report with transparency & explain process
- Role model best use of latest technology
- Show up with authenticity
- Use personal energy for business performance vs. personal gain
- Recognise and quickly act on changes

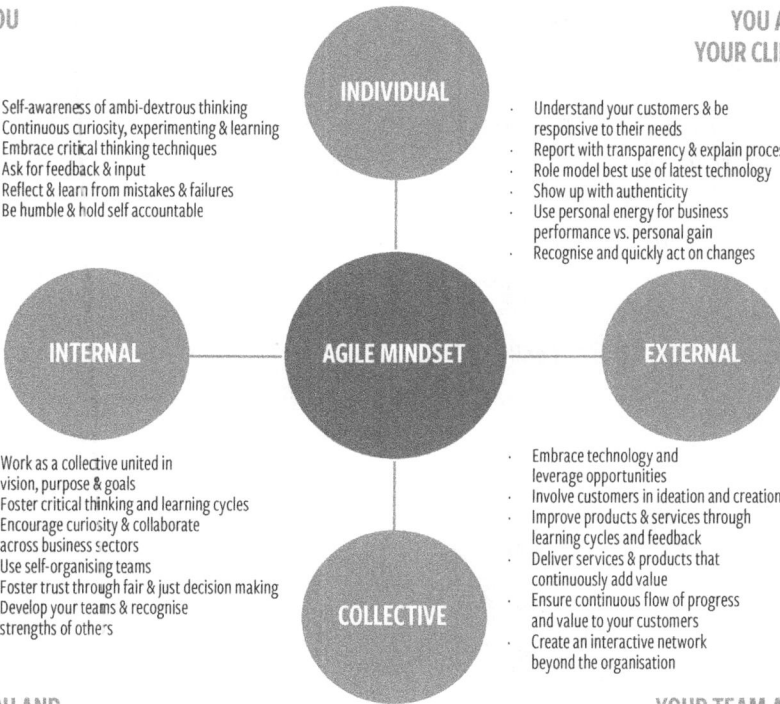

INTERNAL

AGILE MINDSET

EXTERNAL

- Work as a collective united in vision, purpose & goals
- Foster critical thinking and learning cycles
- Encourage curiosity & collaborate across business sectors
- Use self-organising teams
- Foster trust through fair & just decision making
- Develop your teams & recognise strengths of others

COLLECTIVE

- Embrace technology and leverage opportunities
- Involve customers in ideation and creation
- Improve products & services through learning cycles and feedback
- Deliver services & products that continuously add value
- Ensure continuous flow of progress and value to your customers
- Create an interactive network beyond the organisation

YOU AND
YOUR TEAM

YOUR TEAM AND
YOUR CLIENT

Agile mindset model

I've used this model with clients as a temperature check to explore not just how well they're doing agile but also how much awareness and development of an agile mindset is present in individuals and teams. The model is simple but not simplistic. The best way to work with the model is to go through each quadrant and evaluate the different levels of mindset, putting the right steps in place and making the necessary changes.

If you have people who work in silos, or you find that you're stuck, or your clients don't see your progress, check the model to find out in which quadrant the issues show up. The framework is not the solution but a tool to gauge where you're agile and where you need to make changes.

These words from Kent Beck are worth remembering: 'The vagueness of the term agile can be a deterrent. Asking "Are we doing it right?" (or the more likely scenario—telling someone else "You're not doing it right!") is not a very valuable question. "Are we learning all we can?" and "What do we need to change to most benefit our company's goals?" have a lot more impact. If agility is a mindset, then measures of correctness don't really apply.'

> IT'S NOT THE STRONGEST OF THE SPECIES THAT SURVIVES, NOR THE MOST INTELLIGENT THAT SURVIVES. IT IS THE ONE THAT IS MOST ADAPTABLE TO CHANGE.'
>
> —CHARLES DARWIN

One aspect of a VUCA world accelerated by the Covid-19 crisis is constant, and that's change. As leaders, not only do we need to manage change and react to changing environments but we also need to actively lead change: we must anticipate change and lead with intention, strategy and effective communication. With many aspects of our personal and business lives being impacted by things that are out of our control on almost a daily or weekly basis, we often feel like we're playing catch-up.

I work with clients in the travel and hospitality industries. The constant changes to health advice, lockdowns, closures, international travel warnings, and opening and closing of borders puts huge pressure on their leadership teams and employees.

I coached a regional leadership team in the aviation industry, helping them lead their people remotely through the best part of 2020. They still face change daily and need to be nimble and agile. When we're under pressure, sound structures and simple processes are helpful to keep us on track and pave the way to putting the right measures in place. I taught the aviation team how to use the ADKAR (by Prosci) model to lead change consistently and with agility.

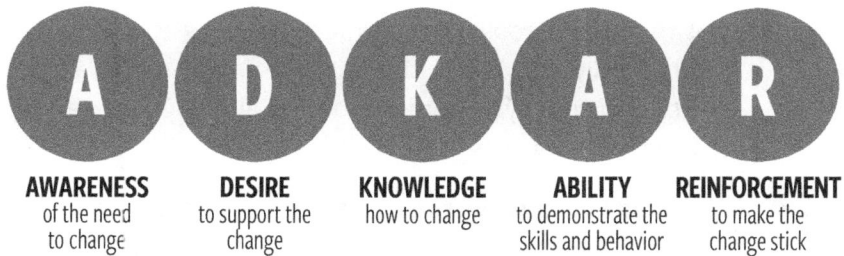

AWARENESS
of the need
to change

DESIRE
to support the
change

KNOWLEDGE
how to change

ABILITY
to demonstrate the
skills and behavior

REINFORCEMENT
to make the
change stick

Leading change is a process. The ADKAR model helps leaders build stages of change and communicate effectively with team members and stakeholders. Change happens at an individual level and helps facilitate change. ADKAR focuses on allowing you to come up with activities that will drive individual change and achieve organisational goals. The model provides clear goals and outcomes for change-management activities. The ADKAR model explained:

- Awareness of the need for change: This is the *why* of the change: the business reason and a goal for early communication. In times of crisis, when we can't anticipate change as we usually do, it's important to have a finger on the pulse. We need to be able to create awareness quickly and communicate with transparency when explaining the *why*. Your communication channels are important here. How fast can you react and inform?

- Desire to make the change happen: This is about personal decisions: the what's-in-it-for-me question. You want people to engage with and participate in change, so you have to gauge their desire to change and also anticipate resistance. This is your opportunity to get buy-in.

- Knowledge about how to change: This is about the how-to. This stage is about more than information. Here we demonstrate the skills, and start with training and coaching new skills and processes.

- Ability to change: This stage is all about implementation. It goes further than simply knowing how to do something. We want to enable people to implement the skills and processes into their daily work and business. It's about realisation, and we have to ensure they have the resources and ongoing training, feedback and coaching.

- Reinforcement to retain the change: This last stage is all about sustaining the change, making it stick. It's about creating habits, adapting measurements and agreeing on what success looks like.

So, how does this model work? How can you use this framework? Go through all the stages from A to R and list the level of each stage for your change. For example, for awareness you could list the reasons why you believe the change is necessary. Then review those reasons and rate the degree to which your people are aware of them (you could even rate them). Then put practical steps in place to increase awareness.

Repeat this process for all the steps in a linear way. Highlight areas where you still have work to do with your teams, and create smart goals and a plan for each stage.

Once you have worked through ADKAR with your people you will want to hear the following from them:

A   I understand why ...
D   I've decided to ...
K   I know how to ...
A   I'm unable to ...
R   I'll continue to ...

'THE BEST CHANGE COMES AS A RESULT
OF INDIVIDUALS REALISING THEY NEED
TO CHANGE.'

—DEAN SHARESKI

SKILL 8: COMPLEX PROBLEM-SOLVING

Problem-solving is the process of finding solutions to difficult or complex issues. The basis for solving a problem is to look at the problem from different angles and think about it critically before jumping into action to solve it. If we do critical thinking well we get better at solving complex problems.

'BEWARE OF PEOPLE PREACHING SIMPLE
SOLUTIONS TO COMPLEX PROBLEMS.
IF THE ANSWER WAS EASY, SOMEONE
MORE INTELLIGENT WOULD HAVE
THOUGHT OF IT A LONG TIME AGO—
COMPLEX PROBLEMS INVARIABLY
REQUIRE COMPLEX AND DIFFICULT
SOLUTIONS.'

—STEVE HERBERT

Leaders who make knee-jerk decisions are often those who feel under pressure to have all the answers immediately. There is so much change happening, and so quickly, that leaders need to adapt to that speed and come up with fast decisions. There is a time and place for fast, confident decisions and just getting things done, but I would encourage leaders to step back and take the time to get more information, include and involve their teams, create and test possible solutions before making any decisions.

Are you quick to make decisions? Do you weigh up the pros and cons and just get on with it? Or are you someone who takes their time, considers multiple possibilities and goes back and forth until a decision has to be made? Most of us have a natural preference when it comes to the pace of our decision-making. Making better decisions is not just about speed; it's also about applying skills and a process that includes critical thinking (CT).

'Critical thinking will become the second most important skill for employees by 2020', claimed the World Economic Forum in their 2016 'Future of Jobs' report. We have moved from the manual worker in the industrial age to the knowledge worker in the digital age. While many people continue to work with their hands, the number of so-called knowledge workers is increasing. This is only one reason why critical thinking is in demand today more than ever before.

When you were to ask leaders at random if they practise critical thinking the answer would almost certainly be yes, of course. But if you were to challenge that answer, it might turn out that the leaders in question might not do quite as well as they think.

One of best critical thinkers I have worked with is a senior leader in the aviation industry. Basically, she questions *everything*, including her own assumptions. She has a process of pressure-testing her team's arguments so that when she is challenged in the boardroom, her critical thinking makes the strategies stand solid. This doesn't just make her look good; it also has a positive effect on her team and creates a critical-thinking culture.

Given the ever-increasing time pressure many people are under, leaders often jump to conclusions based on the available evidence, but fail to reason through the pressing issues carefully enough. Or they choose the evidence that supports their already formed beliefs, which of course are their implicit biases. Paul Gibbons, in his book *Impact*, goes a step further:

'While debiasing sounds as if it's about thinking, people do their best thinking when centred, mindful and emotionally safe. So paradoxically in our technological age, thinking better depends on emotions.'

Gibbons sees the foundation of critical thinking as 'being' before 'thinking'. In other words, it's just as important to have a process as it is to have the right attributes and soft skills. He states that critical thinkers are reflective, self-aware, disciplined, active, sceptical, liberated, humble, agnostic, statistical and scientific. I encourage you to consider a gap analysis in your team or business, and apply relevant training and coaching in some of these areas.

Critical thinking for better decision-making

Critical thinking doesn't just help us make better decisions; it also helps us approach problems in different ways instead of relying on a single approach. It makes us better and more inclusive leaders as we appreciate other peoples' views and ideas, which in turn empowers our teams.

> IN LIGHT OF THE FUTURE OF WORK AND AI, CRITICAL THINKING IS INVALUABLE TO GOVERN SMART MACHINES.'
>
> —PAUL GIBBONS

Critical thinking, a process of reasoning through logic, saves time as we teach ourselves how to filter and prioritise essential information. Critical thinking makes us better listeners, solves problems more effectively, and achieves the best results. Critical thinking skills:

- Diversify thought: Consider other people's experiences and opinions, and recognise and question all possible conclusions before making decisions. You don't have to be right all the time. Accept other options that might not agree with your own preconceived ideas.

- Self-regulation: Leave your emotions out of the equation. Approach arguments and conversations with objectivity and focus on the issue at hand. You're making a decision and solving a problem, and while that probably impacts other people and yourself, it's still just a problem.

- Ask questions and listen well: Before jumping to conclusions, ask open questions to determine what something means and what is being communicated. Ask open questions to interpret, and listen to understand, not just to reply. Create space in your mind to take on information, content, diagrams, behaviours and verbal cues before categorising and judging.

- Question assumptions: Question all possible outcomes and arguments. Explore arguments on a deeper level and ask to see evidence of the possible solutions and outcomes. Analytical skills strive to identify all the assumptions, reasons, themes, and evidence used in making an argument or explanation. It's like pressure-testing assumptions and arguments, and evaluating whether they will hold.

- Reason through logic: Pay close attention to the chain of logic constructed by a particular argument. Evaluate whether the argument is supported by evidence at every point. Do all pieces of evidence build on each other to produce a sound conclusion?

- Inference: Consider consequences for various options and evaluate if those consequences are certain, probably or possible. While sound inference relies on accurate information, you have to draw your conclusions from what you have, e.g. hypothesis or analogical reasoning.

Critical thinking may sound complex, but it's a crucial skill in everyone's team and business. Maybe if we replaced the word 'critical' with 'smart' and became smarter thinkers and better decision makers, we could get more buy-in from the people around us.

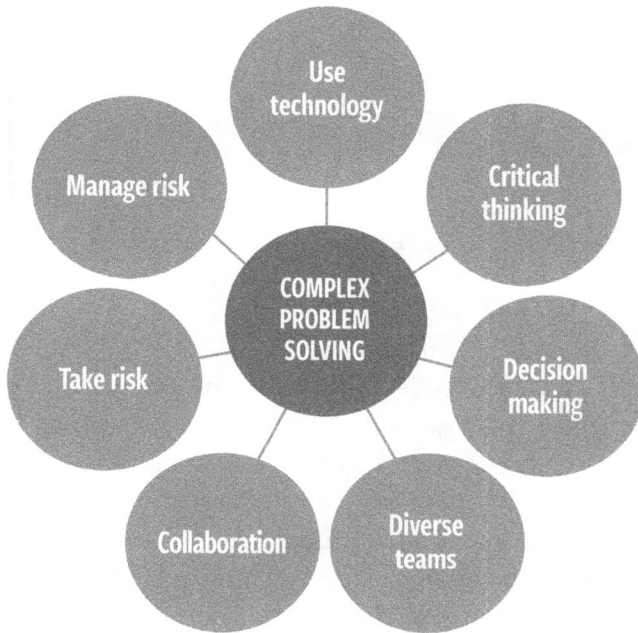

Complex problem solving

There are several factors you have to consider when solving complex problems as a group, not just decision making. You and your team must be willing to apply critical thinking and collaboration, and you need to be aware of the diversity of skills and thinking in the group. Decide what kind of technology you will need to support your problem solving processes, and weigh up taking risks and managing risks. These steps don't happen in a linear fashion: they are all part of complex problem solving activities all of the time.

> DIVERSE GROUPS OF PROBLEM-SOLVERS
> OUTPERFORMED THE GROUPS OF
> THE BEST INDIVIDUALS AT SOLVING
> COMPLEX PROBLEMS. THE REASON:

THE DIVERSE GROUPS GOT STUCK LESS
OFTEN THAN THE SMART INDIVIDUALS,
WHO TENDED TO THINK SIMILARLY.'

—SCOTT E PAGE

SKILL 9: ADAPTABILITY

Adaptability is a core leadership skill in the workplace of the 21st century. In March 2021 I was in a room full of executives at a Women in Leadership Conference in Melbourne, moderating one of the breakout sessions about leading the future. I asked the women to name one thing they did in 2020 that they never thought they'd have to do. The replies came hard and fast, and were fascinating. *Making my dining table my office workstation. Home schooling my children. Wearing Ugg boots every day. Working by myself for months without physically seeing my colleagues. Hiring people I'd never met. Making people redundant via Zoom.*

They were all experiences that couldn't be more removed from the way we normally work, raise our children and live our lives. Whole workforces began to work from home in early 2020 and people adapted well, because they had to.

‘THE WORLD IS BECOMING A FASTER
CHANGING AND MORE TURBULENT PLACE
FOR ORGANISATIONS AND THE NECESSITY
TO ADAPT HAS NEVER BEEN GREATER.'

—JACOB MORGAN

If 2020 taught us one thing it was the fact that change is the only constant. I have had countless conversations with leaders who are reflecting on the challenges they now face: rapid change, unpredictable environments, the challenge of predicting trends and development, recent restructures and workplace changes, and impacted markets.

> ' AND THE MOST SUCCESSFUL PEOPLE ARE THOSE WHO ACCEPT AND ADAPT TO CONSTANT CHANGE. THIS ADAPTABILITY REQUIRES A DEGREE OF FLEXIBILITY AND HUMILITY MOST PEOPLE CAN'T MANAGE.'
>
> —PAUL LUTUS

We experience change at a personal level, and I find that people who have a high amount of adaptability skills are at the forefront when it comes to leading well into the future. We know that 2021 and beyond are going to be tough, with a continuing high degree of uncertainty and ongoing change. Adaptability is the ability to act on signals; however, change can be perceived as a threat by the brain, which puts us into a fight-or-flight mode. When we're faced with unexpected shifts we often shut down. But fighting against something or hoping everything will work out by itself is not the answer.

As we know, hope is not a plan: we need to be intentional about change. A McKinsey report recognises the importance of adaptability to thrive in the future of work: 'Adaptability is the key to thriving in the future world of work as technologies change, employees rethink what they want from work, and customer expectations rise ever higher. All require a different set of skills, but one that will keep shifting. Add to this the Covid-19 pandemic that has disrupted our usual working routines, and it is little wonder that business leaders cite higher levels of uncertainty and anxiety. We cannot know what the future holds.'[30]

Start with a clear and positive mindset. In a crisis, fear can be overwhelming. Negative stories can quickly become part of your mental script: *The world's going to end. I'll lose my job. The company is going to go under.* Apply a growth mindset and change the stories: *This is a temporary situation. We've always been faced with unexpected change. I have the support to make a change.*

It's not just about thinking in a positive way. It's about gaining clarity about what you can and can't change, and celebrating success and progress. This will create capacity and confidence. Adaptability in times of crisis and ambiguity is particularly important, as it will enable you to see the opportunities and not just the struggle.

Adaptability is not a personality trait; it's a behavioural skill and can be learned. The high number of people shifting to remote work, home schooling their children, and adapting to completely new environments is testimony to this.

When facing rapid, constant change, plan in small steps. Don't think about the whole twelve months ahead if you can only impact the next three. Things will change along the way again, and being adaptable means constantly adapting to changing circumstances. Be okay with sitting in discomfort and act anyway, without waiting for things to be okay or for you to feel happy. Embrace being outside your comfort zone and see it as your learning zone.

The five main areas of adaptability in the workplace:

1. Read signals and act on them: Cultivate the ability to read signals of external change and translate and decode them quickly. Refine your antenna for gauging external environments. Make sure your people are connected to the outside world, updated on news and trends, and feel psychologically safe to raise signals. Act swiftly and evaluate the impact of the change, and evaluate the strategy your teams or organisation need to put in place. Don't procrastinate; move forward.

2. Be open to experimentation: Just like change, experimentation happens at a personal level. Encourage curiosity in your teams and organisation; foster a culture where people can ask questions and challenge the status quo from a curiosity point of view, not to criticise someone. Involve everyone in experimentation; don't leave it to the innovation department.

   Many of my clients are running constant brainstorming sessions, mini-consulting projects and hackathons, and keep innovating. Make sure your leaders have a high tolerance for failure; not every new idea or product is an instant success. An idea can often form the basis for critical thinking and finding solutions that no one thought of before.

3. Communicate and mobilise: Experiencing change feels similar to the grieving process. In fact, Dr Elizabeth Kubler-Ross's five stages of grief have been translated to something called 'the change curve'. Unexpected shifts first cause people to feel shock, then go into denial, and then experience depression before they start to experiment and finally integrate.

   Although we seek fast adaptability, we also need to understand the stages people go through when experiencing rapid change in order to plan the most impactful communication. There's no point in training people while they're in shock. Apply empathy and compassion first, let people go through depression, coach them and give them as much information and transparency as you can. As soon as the energy goes up and they're are ready to experiment, that's when you can train and implement. The curve can be one day or three months. You will know.

4. Expect accountability, and focus: Change and uncertainty can trigger weird thoughts and emotions. Resist getting caught up in the media or organisational narrative of blaming people and dramatising context. Stay focused and help your people avoid getting distracted by news, gossip or social media. Focus on

the things you can change, not the things that are out of your control. Be specific and put these things in two columns if you need clarity. When you focus on the things you are in control of you can ask for accountability, and put plans and feedback structures into place accordingly.

5. Adapt or change: When external change comes hard and fast, remember to keep your strategies flexible. You probably recall the back and forth with government regulations in 2020 during the course of several different lockdowns over a number of months: first moving your workforce home, then back to the office, then home again. Nothing is permanent or set in stone. Apply this knowledge to all of your strategies. A strategy is a plan of action designed to achieve certain goals. As the goal posts change, learn to adapt strategies with an agile and flexible approach.

'REVERSING THE OBVIOUS ADAPTION OPENS UP POSSIBILITIES. EVEN JUST SPEAKING THE OPPOSITE OF THE PREVAILING WISDOM OUT LOUD CAN CREATE OPPORTUNITIES.'

—MAX MCKEOWN

SKILL 10: EMBRACE TECHNOLOGY

Being tech savvy is a necessary leadership skill in a hybrid world and the future of work. The current global shift into hybrid workplaces has had a substantial effect on organisations, which have had to pick up their pace to realise digital transformation. Leaders around the globe don't just have to work with new technologies; they also need to embrace the new digital approach to collaboration and communication. They need to lead their organisations in a quest to understand the impact certain technologies might have on their business, people and clients. Leaders don't have to become tech experts, but they do have to become tech savvy and digitally fluent.

> 'MILLENNIALS' TECH AND GLOBAL SAVVY WILL MAKE THEM INSTRUMENTAL IN SHAPING OUR MOBILE FUTURE WORLDWIDE.'
>
> —BRAD D SMITH

With a more diverse workforce—more than seventy percent of leaders are millennials and Generation Z—organisations need to invest in upgrading their technology now. According to Microsoft, sixty-eight percent of workers use their digital devices in the workplace. Employees want to be empowered by technology that helps reduce the time gap in solving critical issues, ensures faster deliveries for clients, and improves professional networks for organisations. Leaders of all ages need to be able to evaluate whether or not their current technology is fit for purpose.

Throughout the last few months, leaders have been asking how to keep their teams focused and motivated during the crisis, and how to lead their remote teams well while keeping them connected. The answer of consistent communication, clear expectations, empowerment through projects, and reward-and-recognition programs has to go hand in hand with leaders embracing technology and leading a digitalised approach in a hybrid world.

How to become tech savvy

If you want to become more tech savvy, start by losing your fear of something going wrong or thinking you need a detailed instruction

---

manual. Explore, jump in, try it out and be curious. No one is being asked to code. It's all about application, and simply using the technology can help you to learn about the application. Apply the mindset of exploring the best technology for your organisation, employees and clients. Technology shapes the way your teams collaborate, communicate and stay productive.

Productivity has increased for some organisations whose people work from home, whereas other organisations have seen a decrease. The fact is that technology impacts productivity, so as a leader it's your job to explore and choose the digital approach that is right for your environment.

> ‘TOMORROW'S LEADERS WILL NEED TO HAVE A TECHNOLOGY FLUENCY THAT LETS THEM ANTICIPATE OPPORTUNITIES AND THREATS, DISTINGUISH HYPE FROM CREDIBLE, AND EMBRACE TRANSFORMATIVE POSSIBILITIES.'
>
> —MICHAEL TIPSORD

Be mindful of the role that technology plays, and invest in training and timely rollouts. Digital transformation is less about technology than it is about people. You can purchase any type of technology, but the ability to adapt to an increasingly digital future depends on developing skills and future-proofing your employees' potential. I always used to say, 'Your CRM and database are only as good as the data put in by your people, no matter how nifty the application is.'

The five steps you can take to embrace digitalisation and become a tech-savvy leader:

Step 1   *Explore and be curious: Jump right in and try out new apps or software applications. Use tools like YouTube, blogs, podcasts and TED Talks, which can provide an overview of new technology and how it can best be applied.*

Step 2   *Surround yourself with tech-savvy people: Build a network of tech-savvy people in your own team and in your tribe. You want people to be able to answer questions, make recommendations and solve problems quickly. Make sure you ask the right questions. As a leader, you don't have to be the expert, but you do need to look at the opportunity technology offers your team and organisation.*

Step 3   *Get your team involved: You're moving into a hybrid world where you may have to disrupt yourself and your products and services, and there's no better time for getting your team members on board. Start by letting them lead projects with the goal of implementing new technologies and digitalising your organisation. Tip: Ask your young millennials and GenZ's.*

Step 4   *Focus on productivity: Productivity has become a focus point in the hybrid world. Explore how digitalisation and new technology can help make teams and employees work more productively. Don't just use technology for technology's sake. What can the tool replace that is no longer available to your teams? Your systems need to be integrated and work together.*

Step 5   *Don't forget soft skills: Technology is only as good as the people using it. Make sure you have buy-in from your teams and that the implementation is supported by all departments. Allow people to be trained to use the new tools and enable your leaders for success. Lead by example and use technology well.*

SKILL 11: VISION AND FORESIGHT

Vision is not just about having a plan. Vision means designing what your future will look like, and then acting upon that design. Strategic plans, to-do lists and change documents often emerge when teams get together to create or renew the vision for an organisation, but what they need is a creative process to paint a picture of their ideal future. Professor John Kotter describes it like this: 'Without a sensible vision, a transformation effort can easily dissolve into a list of confusing and incompatible projects that can take the organisation in the wrong direction or nowhere at all.'

> 'A LEADER MUST POSSESS CREDIBILITY, IMAGINATION, ENTHUSIASM, VISION, FORESIGHT, A SENSE OF TIMING, A PASSION FOR EXCELLENCE AND BE WILLING TO SHARE.'
>
> —WILLIAM ROSENBERG

To be able to envision your future you need to develop foresight, which is also called 'visioning'. Visioning is a process whereby people collectively design a vision of what the ideal future could look like. When you create your vision, stay away from going into planning or problem-solving mode. I recommend using visual aids like vision boards (in the virtual world you can use platforms like Mural), creating both visuals and a narrative to create your ideal future. Tap into your group's emotions and encourage them to use storytelling to describe what the envisioned world looks like, and what, for example, future clients are feeling and doing. Remember the vision Microsoft had of a personal computer in every home.

'DEVELOPING A VISION IS AN EXERCISE OF BOTH THE HEAD AND THE HEART, IT TAKES SOME TIME, IT ALWAYS INVOLVES A GROUP OF PEOPLE, AND IT IS TOUGH TO DO WELL.'

—DAVID KOTTER

Creating a vision that is closely connected to the purpose of your organisation requires not only envisioning the future but also thinking *into* the future. Foresight requires observing trends, pulling behavioural insights and data into the visioning process, and identifying inflection points. Mark W Johnson describes this process as 'early signs of disruption'.

Once you have created your vision, pressure-test it. Ask yourself if everyone can clearly see what the future will look like. Will it be possible to draw clients, employees and stakeholders into the vision? The vision has to be achievable, so you need to decide whether it's feasible and you have the resources to achieve it.

SKILL 12: MOBILISE

We need to mobilise to lead the future. Mobilisation can be generally defined as organising the required or planned resources, which can include people or tools and other equipment, for a specific purpose. Mobilising goes beyond leading change as we switch our view from individuals and teams to cultures of the entire organisation or even the whole world. Mobilising means large-scale, sustainable change involving large groups of people. When we mobilise, we become change makers. Then we get other people involved and inspire *them* to become change makers.

Mobilising reminds me of large flocks of birds migrating thousands of kilometres to settle in environments that help them thrive in a more suitable environment for some time. In the dry centre of Australia we have Lake Eyre, which only fills with water twice each century, but when it does millions of birds migrate there from Asia. Mobilising teams in the business world is, of course, much more complex and deliberate, but this natural behaviour shows us the value of purpose when motivating people in large numbers to change their behaviour.

The challenges with mobilisation often come down to a lack of employee engagement. According to an ongoing Gallup survey in the United States, fourteen percent of workers are 'actively disengaged'; a definition that includes those who have miserable work experiences and spread their unhappiness to their colleagues. According to Gallup, even its highest rate of employee engagement—those who are highly involved in, enthusiastic about, and committed to their work and workplace—is only thirty-eight percent. You can have all the visions, plans and structures in the world, but if you can't mobilise your workforce your vision will remain just that, a vision.

Most people are not intrinsically against change, but they want to be involved and connected to the purpose behind it. A restructure, which so many businesses are going through right now, has a different meaning to the shareholder than it does to the junior manager.

In his book *Impact*, Pau Gibbons writes: 'We want people engaged and inspired because engagement and inspiration are human goods in their own right, not because it will make our enterprises more efficient or profitable.'

Organisations and leaders need to engage with their employees because they care what those people feel and think. This is not about organisational goals or standards of delivering services. It's about how we get there and what individuals need to make the change.

If we want to mobilise people and become change agents, we need to understand how to change behaviour. Methods like influencing or persuasion won't suffice, and reward schemes are effective in the short term only. Gibbons talks about 'neo behaviourism', where we humanise the workplace, care about what people think and feel, use a coaching approach and ask questions to empower people, listen to resistance, and ask more questions.

In an earlier chapter I talked about how our values (what we think to be right) and beliefs (what we think to be true) drive our behaviour, but Gibbons states that it's often the other way around: we believe how we behave. I find that fascinating, as it opens up new ways of changing behaviour, one of the fundamentals of making mobilisation successful. We need to replace bad habits with good habits to affect our culture in order to mobilise it.

For example, if you wanted to mobilise your people to innovate creative future solutions but your company culture was riddled with unproductively structured and facilitated meetings, simply inspiring people to change wouldn't be enough. You would need to change the habit of having unproductive meetings to having productive meetings. For example, you could make the meetings shorter, suggest that people stand rather than sit, make sure there was always a purpose and an agenda, and train your people so they know how to workshop. Gibbons says we need to 'disrupt the conduct of (unproductive) rituals'.

Mobilising requires people to buy into a vision and engage in the change required to achieve that vision. As we know from using coaching approaches, the most impactful way to increase engagement is empowerment. Involve your people in creating your vision instead of letting the executive team come up with one that mostly serves stakeholders and shareholders. Ask your people what behaviours are necessary to achieve the vision.

One practical example is the vision of the hybrid workplace. We already know that people want flexibility when returning to work. Upskill your leaders to have coaching conversations with your employees to find out what they think and feel, and use models like the time-and-place model to work out the best options. Do this across the company and get collective buy-in for the solutions that work best for the majority of your workforce.

Change in the digital age means being ready to embrace technology, which is an essential skill for leaders who want to mobilise their workforce. People can become overwhelmed if too much technology is being pushed on them, and a lack of training and best practice makes technology inefficient. For example, many organisations have added software like Microsoft Teams for day-to-day use, but without guidelines and boundaries employees can get lost in channels, teams, emails and instant messages.

Instead of making a quick top-down decision when purchasing technology, ask your teams what they need in order to work towards the vision. Embrace technology in order to take practical steps.

For your people to change effectively and become change agents, they need to have access to self-development, and it has to start at the top. It's the soft skills that matter. When was the last time your executives had coaching and training for their own development? If you can't remember, make sure you start implementing learning and development from the highest level, right down to your most junior people.

Development opportunities increase engagement, and engagement is what is needed most to mobilise. As Peter Senge says: 'People do not resist change; they resist being changed.'

I have developed a mobilising framework with six key strategies:

1. Envisioning and foresight: Mobilising is more than imagining a future where we run successful and profitable organisations. According to Mark W Johnson, it's 'about identifying potential inflection points in your industry and the timeframe when they are likely to occur—the early signals of disruption—and then you develop a broader picture of that environment'. Envision how you will help your clients in that environment and whom you will compete with.

2. Trust and buy-in: Create psychological safety throughout the organisation to increase the level of trust so people can share ideas no matter how outrageous they may seem. You want your people to be creative and to innovate, challenge the status quo and ask questions that change the future. Empower them to own and deliver ideas and projects. This will hit the engagement scale directly.

3. Mobilise leaders at all levels: Don't confine your future vision to the executive team or project groups. It has to happen throughout the entire organisation and be shared continuously. Make employee engagement a priority on all levels of the organisation. Adopt a leaders-create-leaders culture where empowerment and encourage-ment, rather than winning and acknowledgement, are the drivers.

4. Accountability and leading by example: There is nothing worse than being asked to work on a project by a manager who never follows up. People want to be held accountable, receive feedback and see the fruits of their work. Organisations with a high level of accountability are significantly more productive and successful than those without.

5. Collaboration and co-creation: Innovation doesn't happen in a vacuum. We need to rely on our collective wisdom, experience and cognitive diversity to solve complex problems. Rather than creating silos and isolated business areas, encourage your teams to collaborate and co-create across disciplines.

6. Embrace technology: Equip your people with the technology they need to innovate, collaborate and communicate. Workforces need to be mobile and able to work remotely while staying connected. Technology needs to help and not hinder people to be productive. Don't leave it to the IT department. Embracing technology doesn't mean you have to be an expert; look at it as an opportunity that technology offers your workforce.

> 'LEADERSHIP IS ABOUT SETTING A DIRECTION. IT'S ABOUT CREATING A VISION, EMPOWERING AND INSPIRING PEOPLE TO WANT TO ACHIEVE THE VISIONS AND ENABLING THEM TO DO IT WITH ENERGY AND SPEED THROUGH EFFECTIVE STRATEGY. IN ITS MOST BASIC SENSE, LEADERSHIP IS ABOUT MOBILISING A GROUP OF PEOPLE TO JUMP TO A BETTER FUTURE.'
>
> —JOHN P KOTTER

CONCLUSION

The speed of change, uncertainty of world events, and increasingly automated work processes can be daunting and paralysing. You may feel that you have to change everything you're doing now so you can cope with the future of work, but the fundamentals of leadership are still the same; leading self and leading others, and putting the human at the centre when it comes to creating the future is still where the focus should be. The overall mode of leadership *is* changing, however, and that's what you need to respond to.

I have written this book to give you context about what is happening in the world right now and how that impacts you, your team members and business. My intention is not to frighten you, but to make you aware of what most people are experiencing; it's about realising that change is inevitable, and understanding how that change impacts you right now.

I have focused on the foundation skills of emotional intelligence and building resilience because those are the skills most needed when envisioning the future and mobilising the workforce. Only after emphasising the importance of these have I discussed the skills that are specifically needed in a world of AI, and continuing questions about the future of work. As leaders, we cannot expect to digitalise a whole company without first giving people the skills to come on this journey with us, and communicate with empathy.

I encourage you to check which of the 5 Megatrends are impacting you and your team or business the most. Make some notes, and have conversations with the people around you about how they see the reality. Leaders don't know it all, and still need other people's perspectives.

The team-member engagement model is a fantastic tool to gauge exactly where you are on your journey to lead the future, and shows you what to focus on next. You might find you are closer than you think.

Growing exponentially is all about focusing on your strengths. This book should help you discover what you're already doing well, and which of the 12 Skills you need to revisit and strengthen, and which are new to you or your organisation. You could use KSS (keep doing, stop doing, start doing) to write a plan to develop the skills that are most needed right now to lead the future. Working through the 12 Skills doesn't have to be a linear process, but it may help if you start with Lead Self.

Lead the Future is intended to be inspirational through its stories, educational through its models and megatrends, and practical by giving you the 12 Skills necessary to lead the future and not be intimated by it.

I would love to hear how you're getting on with implementing the skills and leadership development interventions. Please reach out to me to share your stories and experiences; you can email me at jessica@intactteams.com

WORK WITH JESSICA

In a world where change has become the only constant, the focus to lead change has to be on human skills since they shape the way we embrace automation and disruption, and create the workplace of the 21st century. We need to focus on the necessary soft skills that drive teams and organisations through increased engagement.

With over twenty-five years of corporate experience in Europe and Asia-Pacific, Jessica Schubert has become one of the most sought-after leadership experts. She is the founder of Intact Teams, a global leadership practice that helps organisations develop their leaders in a quest to create workplace cultures where people are happy *and* productive. Just some of the clients she has worked with include British Airways, ANZ Bank, Grill'd Healthy Burgers, Fidessa, Ernst & Young, UK Homeoffice, Elders Insurance.

Jessica is an experienced executive coach, team coach and facilitator. Using her vast international expertise in leadership and managing cross-cultural teams, she custom designs and facilitates leadership workshops across all industry sectors, be it in person or in a virtual setting.

Teams, individuals and organisations face different challenges. Jessica's mission is to listen, understand, and tailor learning solutions that fit the relevant people and their organisational goals. Her steps to help create high performing teams:

Conversation: Listen and understand challenges

Consult: Suggest tailored learning solutions

Co-create: Include leaders in the design process

Coach: Deliver, facilitate and coach

Consider: Seek feedback and go back to conversation

Jessica understands all facets of leadership. She leverages her experience of dealing with power dynamics and organisational complexities and blends it with proven leadership models, coaching theories and adult learning principles.

High-performing teams and leaders is where Jessica specialises; she helps them step into new roles, create high-performing teams, manage stakeholders, and have tough conversations with ease.

Jessica was born and educated in Germany, but has made Australia her home. She enjoys the outdoors, is an avid surfer, and loves spending her weekends visiting Melbourne's art galleries, and photographing the city's unique laneways and eclectic people.

Contact Jessica on jessica@intactteams.com for a free consultation, or check out her website: www.intactteams.com

ENDNOTES

1   https://www.forbes.com/sites/jeroenkraaijenbrink/2018/12/19/what-does-vuca-really-mean/?sh=2a1affbd17d6
2   McCrindle 2019
3   https://www.weforum.org/agenda/2016/01/the-fourth-industrial-revolution-what-it-means-and-how-to-respond/
4   https://hbr.org/2020/09/how-amazon-automated-work-and-put-its-people-to-better-use
5   https://www.mckinsey.com/featured-insights/future-of-work/jobs-lost-jobs-gained-what-the-future-of-work-will-mean-for-jobs-skills-and-wages
6   https://www.pwc.com/us/en/library/covid-19/us-remote-work-survey.html#content-free-1-cbb3
7   https://www.mckinsey.com/business-functions/organization/our-insights/reimagining-the-post-pandemic-organization
8   https://hbr.org/2021/05/how-to-do-hybrid-right
9   https://hbr.org/2021/03/the-state-of-globalization-in-2021

10   https://www.forbes.com/sites/deloitte/2020/01/22/reducing-environ-mental-impact-is-now-a-business-imperative/?sh=6deo17f66cc6

11   https://news.stanford.edu/2021/02/23/four-causes-zoom-fatigue-solutions/

12   https://www.ncbi.nlm.nih.gov/pmc/articles/PMC3105890/

13   https://hbr.org/2019/10/how-engaged-is-your-team-really\

14   https://www.adp.com/-/media/adp/ResourceHub/pdf/ADPRI/ADPRI0102_2018_Engagement_Study_Technical_Report_RELEASE%20READY.ashx

15   https://thesystemsthinker.com/the-art-of-foresight-preparing-for-a-changing-world/

16   https://www.forbes.com/sites/veronikasonsev/2019/11/27/patagonias-focus-on-its-brand-purpose-is-great-for-business/?sh=2ca270d54cb8

17   https://www.infoq.com/articles/what-agile-mindset/

18   https://www.psychologytoday.com/us/blog/living-the-questions/201501/the-heart-effective-leadership

19   https://www.marcusbuckingham.com

20   http://www.viacharacter.org

21   https://www.iecl.com/sorry-need-keep-talking-resilience/

22   https://dradamfraser.com/shop-content/strive

23   https://www.weforum.org/agenda/2016/01/the-10-skills-you-need-to-thrive-in-the-fourth-industrial-revolution/

24   https://www.forbes.com/sites/hvmacarthur/2021/03/13/influencing-the-future-the-most-critical-skill-for-career-success-in-2021--how-to-build-it/?sh=427fef3253a8

25   https://hbr.org/2013/12/building-a-feedback-rich-culture

26   https://www.forbes.com/sites/rodgerdeanduncan/2017/09/23/produc-tive-conflict-is-not-an-oxymoron/?sh=238efa0e4b19

27   https://www.hays.com.au/blog/-/blogs/what-is-a-hybrid-team-and-how-do-i-lead-one-

28   https://www.forbes.com/sites/tracybrower/2021/03/14/wellness-and-the-future-of-work-some-of-the-best-companies-share-their-new-solutions/?sh=3a93f8fe3577

29   www.infoq.com/articles/what-agile-mindset/

30   https://www.mckinsey.com/business-functions/mckinsey-accelerate/our-insights/accelerate-blog/adaptability-and-how-to-future-proof-your-skill-set-for-the-decade-ahead

www.ingramcontent.com/pod-product-compliance
Lightning Source LLC
Chambersburg PA
CBHW060041030426
42334CB00019B/2436